SPLASHING OVER

PRACTICAL ANGER MANAGEMENT FOR CHRISTIANS

MARK IAN THOMPSON

SPLASHING OVER

Editors: MaryBelle Thompson and John Thompson
Co-Editor: Jordan Allan

ISBN-13: 978-1-77069-118-6

Printed in Canada.

Word Alive Press
131 Cordite Road, Winnipeg, MB R3W 1S1
www.wordalivepress.ca

WORD ALIVE PRESS
Just Write!

FSC

Mixed Sources
Cert no. SW-COC-001271
© 1996 FSC

DEDICATION

In 2 Samuel 18:33 King David, upon hearing of the death of his son emits a cry that resonates with parents centuries later – "O my son Absalom! My son, my son Absalom! If only I had died instead of you – O Absalom, my son, my son!"

What is it about a father's love for his son, even as in the case of David, where his son was trying to kill him, that brings such heartbreak when that love is broken? Just as God the Father continues to reach out to us, his lost sons, families since time began have struggled to keep that bond alive. This book is about the anger in relationships that can perpetuate for generations if it is not dealt with by the healing hand of God.

I would like to dedicate this book, the story of my journey which began with my broken relationship with my father, to my family. . .

- *My father and my mother,* now I believe in Jesus' arms - damaged in their own childhood, but doing the best they could

- *My beautiful sister, Valerie,* who has met the many challenges in her life with courage and integrity, always loving me.

- *My blended family,* my many brothers and sisters who in our adulthood, have blessed me so much and made me proud to be their brother

- *My 'adopted' family* – my sisters' and brothers-in-law, and of course, Hazel and Fred, who accepted me, taught me, and loved me as a son.

. . . and especially the family that God in His mercy entrusted to me:

- *My wife MaryBelle*, who saw in me, even as a young man, something that I could not see in myself – someone worth loving. She has loved me for almost 40 years, in richness and in poverty, in sickness and in health, and has encouraged me to seek God's direction and then walked along with me into the adventures..

- *My daughter, Brandy,* my firstborn, a brave soul, stepping out to be the beautiful, kind, talented young woman that God created her to be.

- *My son, John,* a man of adventure, passion, and loyalty who has become my dear friend.

- *My baby, Hazel,* a lovely woman inside and out, who had the courage to stand up to her convictions, teaching the whole family what unconditional love and acceptance are really all about.

Family is the core of my life – my own family, and the families I try to help in my profession as they struggle to get along.

I thank God every day for these people that love me unconditionally and have made my life's journey more than I ever dreamed it could be.

Special Acknowledgments

Those who know me know that I am a man of many limitations. I am the first to admit it. Without the support, encouragement and blessings of many I would never have been able to get this book from it's inception to the finished product you are now holding.

I have attempted to include the names of some of those, but of course there is no way I can include you all as these pages would run on and on.

I would, however, like to acknowledge the special help and support of the following:

- *Pastors Don and Ruth Rousu* for starting me on my journey of healing

- *Pastor Glen Carlson and Pastor Boyd Hopkins* for their vision of the Immanuel Healing Centre, and including me in their vision

- *Pastor Jim Bredeson,* my spiritual advisor and friend

- *Pastor Lucretia van Ommeren-Tabbert,* my friend and encourager

- *Bob and Marie Weigl,* for mapping out the vision for my practice

- *Del and Dee Louis,* for their generosity and belief in my work

- *Curt and Sheila Scheewe* for supporting my professional and personal journey

- *Glen and Linda Vaxvick* for being instrumental in getting this book off the ground

- *My many counselees and students over the years,* who have often taught me as much as I have taught them

- *My co-counselors, Immanuel staff, and fellow Healing Centre workers,* who have helped me run courses, supported my practice, listened to me and encouraged me when I needed it most

- *My fellow missionaries from World Mission Prayer League and the Alliance Academy in Ecuador,* for enriching my life and allowing me to minister to them, while teaching me so much

- *The congregation at Immanuel Lutheran Church of Rosenthal,* comprised of individuals who listen to God, standing by us when things were good and when they were not so good, loving us and praying for us, accepting us just as we were – I will forever be grateful.

- *Natalie Oulette,* bravely doing the first read of the manuscript and giving her valuable input

- *MaryBelle, my wife,* who spent hours pouring over this manuscript, and I must admit, usually getting her own way. She has truly been my partner in all areas of my life.

- *My children* for allowing me to tell their stories to illustrate the impact of anger, and also for their continued encouragement to tell my story. I admit I have taken them on a journey that most will never experience, some of it good and some of it hard. They have become vibrant, kind, loving people who truly do the good they ought to do. What more can a father ask?

- I want to give a special acknowledgment to *my son John.* He believed that I should write this book. Over the space of two years, he encouraged me to take my anger course and make it a book. My son and I are very different people, but through my healing I have learned to appreciate and love the person he is – we have developed a mutual respect and trust for each other that I value so much .I want to thank you, John, for giving me the gift of this book, and for loving me for who I am. You did a fantastic job of keeping me on task, by ultimately putting together a book that I am proud to publish.

And lastly, I want to thank God for the life He has given me – for His grace and mercy in using me to speak into the lives of those suffering from anger.

TABLE OF CONTENTS

1. THE PAIL

The cold winter wind howled as it whipped around the station house. It must have been at least −20 outside. Except for that wind, the house was quiet, too quiet. The drunken curses, screams and screeching accusations were absent, but I wished they were back. The muffled struggle and the slam of the front door were more than I could bear. The only thing I could hear was my little heart beating like a drum in my chest.

It was not an unusual occurrence to have my parents fight like this. He had thrown her out to cool off. Some nights she would just walk down to the bar, and other times she'd break a window to get in. That night, she just lay against the door and called my name to come downstairs to let her in.

The house was completely black, and I was more afraid of passing by my father's room than walking through the darkness. He was crazy when he was drunk. I had tried to let her in before and Dad had grabbed me by the ear — his favourite part of me to get a hold of — and slammed me into the wall until I ran away.

Like any boy, I loved my mom and, more than anything, I wanted to rescue her from my father and from the prairie cold that might kill her if she was outside too long.

I waited in my room in the dark and listened to my mom call for me until I heard my dad's snores. As quietly as I could, I crept through the dark and went down the stairs to the front door. I knew that if he woke up and caught me, I would take the brunt of the violence.

"Mom," I whispered through the crack of the door. "Mom, are you okay?"

"Mark, let your mom in, you need to let your mom in. Be a good boy and let me in." Her words were slurred with the drink, and I could smell her breath through the door.

"Mom, promise me that if I let you in you won't go fight with Dad again." I knew that he would come for me if I let her in.

"I promise I'll be quiet and just go to bed. There ain't gonna be no more trouble tonight."

I started to cry and went for the bolt. As soon as she heard the click, the door flew open against my head and sent my little body smashing back against the wall.

My vision went black for a second as I tried to blink through the pain. The cold air rushed in and woke me up, biting into my bare feet.

She was upstairs in a flash, and I cringed when I heard the door upstairs slam. She started to screech obscenities at him and he murmured to rouse himself from his drunken slumber to fight her off.

In that moment, I could feel something rise in me, an awful feeling of shame, fear and loneliness that would not leave. The tears streamed from my eyes, but it was no use.

In that moment I felt a betrayal of trust that I could not understand and did not have the tools to process. I took that surge

*of emotion and stored it away, deep deep inside myself where I
didn't have to deal with it anymore.*

My pail had begun to fill.

WHAT IS THE PAIL?

Have you ever tried to walk around with a pail of water?
Holding it to one side will throw off your balance, and the
water will start to pick up that uneven motion until it starts
to splash over the edge. In my case, it usually splashes out
all over the most embarrassing places.

In many Third World countries, it is the duty of the
woman to walk miles to the common well to pick up the
water for the day. This ritual is nearly timeless and can be a
fascinating thing to watch. When the women walk back
home with their full pails of water, they have to do so in a
calm and balanced way. If not, they will spill the water or,
even worse, drop the pail.

We, too, carry a pail with us our whole lives, but
instead of carrying it on top of our heads, we carry it in our
subconscious minds, in our memories and in our hearts. We
fill this pail with all of the emotional experiences that we go
through from childhood into old age. The analogy of the
pail is useful to describe the way we hang on to our
experiences and carry them with us into the present, and for
that reason, I will use it for the rest of this book.

Some of the experiences are positive, like the
unconditional love of a family member or friend. That
stored emotion filters into our lives like a watering bucket.
The positive experiences allow us to grow into happy
fulfilled adults.

Yet many of the experiences from our past are full of pain and mistrust and can become toxic over time. Some of that poisonous liquid drains into our lives, giving us feelings of shame, insecurity and inadequacy. Most of that emotion is stored in our pail and becomes a noxious liquid that can splash over in negative expressions when we become unbalanced.

We keep this liquid emotion within us, some of it seeping down into our souls through the holes in the bottom of our pail, but most of it sloshes around just waiting to spill out when we lose our balance. That spilled emotion is like acid, burning those that are closest to us.

That experience of splashing in turn adds more to the pail and, instead of draining out the painful emotion, we just add more. These are the moments when we scream at our partner, spank our kids too hard, demean people we work with or stop talking to our parents for long periods of time. Other times, we push it back inside, making our stored anger even more potent than it was before.

When I became a Christian and gave my heart to Christ, I thought that He would wash me clean. I was convinced that being born again would make me a completely new person.

The truth is that I was born again and the power of my sins was washed away. My heart had been opened to the most amazing truth on earth: unconditional love.

Yet I asked myself, why am I still so filled up with negative thoughts and emotions? If He washed my sins away, then why do I still struggle with keeping balance in my life? Why do I still splash over emotionally in a destructive way?

If you also feel this confusion, then you are not alone in this world. Many wounded Christians feel the frustration of why their anger was not washed away with the rest of their sins when they asked Jesus into their hearts.

What many do not understand is that it is not anger that needs to be washed away. What needs to be drained are the stored emotions of all the past experiences that prevent us from achieving freedom. Those are the things that have become tainted and will continue to taint our personal growth into loving caring human beings. This process takes time and dedication, but it will end in emptying your pail of pain and mistrust.

The flame of anger is not an evil thing in and of itself. The truth is that the fires of anger are the emotional signals that tell us that something has to change. Anger is like a live torch that we carry with us to show that something is wrong. Anger can be used to light up injustice, protect our loved ones or burn down the old corruption in order to make room for new and better things.

When we are not balanced and our pails are too full, the negative emotion will spill out over onto the fire and an explosion will follow, usually with painful repercussions.

We are called on to develop more control over our anger. We are called on to use that anger for personal, social and spiritual change. We are to learn to respond to anger in an assertive modality that reflects the way Jesus responded to anger.

The power of life is choice. To effectively manage and heal our anger issues, we must choose to improve our self-control in order to maintain that healthy emotional balance.

This book is designed to help you look at yourself clearly to see what you have stored in your pail. It will be painful at first to open your eyes to the mess you might find, but it is essential to know *who you are* in order to change *who you will be*. This book will help you see the negative patterns you may have fallen into that keep adding negative emotions to your pail and also to the pails of those around you.

There are ways to change our lives so that we can maintain equilibrium. With proper balance, we won't spill out with personal issues that will hurt our families. There are practical ways to defuse dangerous emotional situations, which will lead you to enact meaningful changes in your life.

This book will also be a tool for those living with angry people, wanting to find real ways to help themselves and their families grow into happiness and trust.

We all have a choice to change the way we react, think and feel about our lives. It is here in front of us now. By making smart Bible-based choices, we can maintain balance and empty the stored emotion in our pails.

All things are possible with Jesus Christ, but we need to find out what needs to be changed and then have the courage to ask Jesus to come into our lives to give us the strength to act.

HEALING PRAYERS

Healing prayers, I believe, are an essential part of the Christian's walk toward wholeness in Christ. We know that

Jesus heals; therefore, it is a given that we ask, and ask often, for Jesus to come into our lives and move us along the road to recovery. The healing prayers that I have included in this book will block the portals that Satan uses to insert himself into our lives and relationships—to take away the cracks that cause us to lose our footing, tip our pails and then splash. With this covering of prayer, Satan is denied the access to come into our lives destroying our peace, our love for others and ourselves, and our ability to become the men and women that God created us to be.

As I cover different aspects of anger in our lives, I have included healing prayers at the end of each section. You can pray these alone, quietly, as you ponder the teachings, or you can ask someone you trust to be there with you as you pray. God will hear you.

God's Word

Romans 8:6 – "The mind of sinful man is death, but the mind controlled by the Spirit is life and peace."

2 Corinthians 10:5 – "We demolish arguments and every pretension that sets itself up against the knowledge of God, and we take captive every thought to make it obedient to Christ."

PRAYER FOR SELF CONTROL

LORD JESUS,
Today I pray for the gift of self-control. It is Yours to give freely, and I desperately need this gift. I ask You, by your Holy Spirit, to infuse me with the

knowledge that I need not lose control when things upset me or do not go my way. Give me the ability to see circumstances through your eyes and not my own, and to remain peaceful and objective in my thoughts and actions. Help me to recognize when I am losing control of my thoughts and actions and to continuously call out to you to give me strength in all areas of my life. AMEN.

Exercise – Self Control

To heal from the wounds we have received, we must reach out to God who gives us peace that passes understanding. Through the power of scripture and the love of Jesus, we can begin to gain control over our lives, which means waking up to the need to take this first step.

The Bible teaches us that we are to actively seek the gift of self–control. If you realize you need the gift of self-control, you can start to seek it out from God asking him in prayer to bless you with that precious fruit.

You might wonder: how can God give us self-control when anger is overtaking our lives?

When I am angry, I will sometimes take a time out and go to a private place to say these scriptures to myself and repeat what they mean until my anger has dissipated and I am back in equilibrium. The Spirit of God enters me and gives me self control. Jesus takes our thoughts captive and makes them obedient to him. Embracing God's will can help me gain control over any emotion.

WHAT IS IN MY PAIL?

"I can't believe she did that." *The panicked thoughts swirled through my mind as I tried to gather my reason for what I'd do next. How could my own sister rat on me like that? Especially since she was the one that thought it would be fun to put rocks on the rails.*

She had said, "Don't worry about it Mark, the trains will just push the rocks off and the sparks are really cool."

We didn't even get that far before someone noticed us. Next thing I know, she's talking to Dad and pointing at me, crying like I made her do it.

Oh no. I can see him drinking from that coffee cup like he's dying of thirst. I know what's in there. It's not coffee. I can smell the rum from here.

Should I run? He'll catch me for sure. Even though I did okay this year at track and field, I know that eventually I'll have to come home. He's gonna beat me bad.

"Are you an idiot? Why are you so stupid?" *His voice shakes the pictures on the office wall as he drags me by the ear inside.*

I glimpse the shocked look of a lady in a green dress outside waiting for the train. She looks as scared as I feel.

The world goes black as he slams my head against the light switch. It shatters and falls to the floor. I follow the pieces into darkness.

Who is Dad talking to? They are certainly giving him a piece of their mind. Are they talking about me? Did someone report Dad?

I hear the warning.

"You can't treat your kids like that, not where people can hear. This is a decent town full of decent folks, and if you don't get

control of your kids and yourself, we'll take this matter to the police and maybe you'll lose them."

It was that social worker Edna that came to the school sometimes. A surge of hope flashes through me. Maybe Dad will stop.

I hear the door of the station house close and there is silence. The tinny sound of a bottle being unscrewed shakes me to my feet. I open the door and see his blank look.

"You shamed me son, now you are going to pay."

My Own Pail

In our formative years, we have no control over what gets put into our pail. We don't know how to set boundaries, and we can't protect ourselves from the ugly things other people splash out onto us and into our pails.

When something evil happens to someone, they might store it so deep inside that it grows roots there. Those turbulent emotions may swell until their pail is so full that it has to spill over the sides. Many pail fillers are parents, teachers and other authorities who often think that they can relieve some of their own pain by passing it on to someone else.

Talking about my own full pail is difficult for me to do publically because admitting to the life I have lead often brings about a deep feeling of shame. I feel responsible for the things that were done to me and even talking about them makes me emotional.

I think that we all need to look closely into our history to see what is in our pail and how it got there. If we can't see the negative emotions we have been storing, then it will be nearly impossible to get rid of them.

For the most part, I was raised in a small country town in a rural part of Canada. After the war, my father Jack married Jean and they had two children together, my sister and me.

My father was respected in the community and worked as a station agent. There are stories about how he would go the extra mile just to drop off a package. He was a handsome man, active in the community and well spoken. Yet there was a darkness in him that no one, including myself, could ever figure out.

I believe that something happened to my father, before World War II or afterwards, that broke him inside. In my younger years, he could hide the ugliness behind a debonair hat and kind eye. But something happened to him in his own life that filled his pail up with negative emotions. The only way that he thought he could survive was by drinking until all the hard edges were gone.

The pail doesn't work like that, though; adding alcohol, drugs or other negative intoxicants to it only makes it more intense, unstable and likely to splash over in violence.

During the day, my father would drink rum from a coffee cup or go down to the Legion and come back home as a mean and nasty drunk. I don't remember the first time he beat me, and I don't like to think about those nightmarish experiences. He would grab me by my ears and slam me into the wall over and over again. To this day, I hate it when anyone goes close to my ears. Sometimes the violence was random and without reason, and other times it was a result of an argument with my mom.

My mother was an attractive woman and, to her, beauty was everything. I felt that she loved my sister more because of her beauty and would praise her for it. I felt that she didn't see or pay attention to me because of my big eyes or funny teeth.

Jean came from an abusive family and was deeply scarred. The love she gave me was also random, at times with the loving embrace of a good mother, and other times she would make me leave the house at meal time without eating because I wasn't wanted there.

My mother was a severe alcoholic and got into terribly violent fights with my father. She seldom protected me from his wrath, and for that reason I felt betrayed and abandoned by her. Jean always told me that while she was pregnant with me, she developed tumours and the only relief for the pain was to drink it away. When she was drunk, she would pick fights with my father or throw casual insults at me.

When I turned seven, my parents got divorced. Their violent fighting and betrayals had pushed our family over the breaking point. When it finally did crack, so did my school life. I failed second grade and felt a great sense of shame at being held back.

My dad remarried soon after, and suddenly our house of four became a house of 14. With so many step brothers and sisters, I felt forgotten and became enmeshed in the anger of a blended family. It seemed like I had to fight for every scrap of food and struggled to find my place in the household. I wore only hand-me-down clothes and had to sleep in a room packed with people. The emotional explosions and abuse I suffered from that household added so much pain to my pail that it is hard for me to quantify it.

In that time period, my mother was promiscuous and had a bad reputation in our small town. When she finally did settle down with one partner, Mike, I became little more than an afterthought in their world. To please her, I would do all of her housework for the day, but she would still kick me out before supper and send me back to the crowded house because she didn't want me around. Again and again, the shame and abandonment that came from her added more negative emotions to my pail and grew into lifelong self-esteem issues.

I have a learning difference that is called dyslexia. I struggled in school, not learning how to read or write until grade four. One of my teachers shamed me in front of the class, mocking other students if they scored lower than me. My home life was such a nightmare that I put everything into school, and by high school, I had decent grades, a girlfriend and played sports. The stinging remarks that questioned my intelligence never left me. I felt like one of those ships that pass other ships in the fog without ever being truly seen for who I really was.

As a teenager, I faced poverty like few North Americans have known. There were times when I was homeless, penniless and had only the clothes on my back. No one wanted me around, and because of my gentle attitude, I was regularly picked on by my siblings. In high school, I had to deal with homelessness and poverty, which still affects me to this day as I constantly worry about money issues.

I started in with a "gang" of similarly wayward boys in the town and found my family there with them. We would drink and smoke, earning bad reputations. Yet they supported me when no one else would, and if I needed somewhere to go, they looked out for me. My gang became my family.

Then one day, my dad got a job in another province and had to relocate. My mother refused to let me live with her, and just like that, the people that supported me were gone from my life. The feeling of leaving the only people that loved me added to my pail, but even then I hoped that maybe it was a chance to start over.

Instead of the fresh start, it became worse than I had ever imagined. My father's drinking and violence became so out of control that he could barely hold down his job. I was so ashamed that any of my friends might see him like that, and they were not invited to come to my house.

At 17, my pail was already full to the brim, and I was looking at splashing out everywhere.

Then one night, everything changed.

It's a Friday night, which means that my dad would be done a case of beer and onto the bottle of wine. I know that by the end of the night, his rum and wine stench will choke out everyone in the house.

It's been a couple years since we'd moved here to Kitimat. His bouts have gotten worse and more regular. I always have to be on my toes.

Just last week, he burst into my room and grabbed me by the hair, yanking me off the chair. I had forgotten to do the dishes earlier, and he paid me my lesson by dragging me backwards to the kitchen. A whole hunk of my hair was ripped out, and the kids in school sure had a laugh.

Just thinking of that makes my blood boil. I gotta get that monster back before he gets me again. I am so sick of his smell, I could just puke thinking of his disgusting odour.

I don't know why I always gotta push his buttons. It's like there's some kind of demon inside me that wants to set him off. One of these days, I'm going to get my chance, and he'll regret ever laying hands on me.

I walk to my stereo and put my favourite LP on. Good old Jimi, he sure can screech out that guitar and it feels just like my rage sliding across that field where the princess kept watch.

"All Along the Watchtower, princess kept a view, while other servants came and went, their foot servants too. Outside in the cool distance, a wildcat did prowl, two riders were approaching, and the wind began to howl."

There it was, the screech of madness that I knew so well in my brain. Quickly, I grab the butter and steak knives I had jammed in my door to replace the broken lock. He is going to try to bust in any second, but these are going stop him dead in his tracks. Hopefully, he's just gonna pass out so I can go out drinking with my friends.

His footsteps thunder down the hall, and his fists beat madly on my door. There is a sudden silence before a deafening crack.

Jack, that out-of-control drunken madman, has thrown his drunken soft body right at the door and busted it wide open. He goes down with the wood like a sack of potatoes.

The impact must have knocked him cold. Serves him right.

I see one of the knives lying there, glinting in the bare bulb light. It's calling to me, that blade, calling for my hand to grip it.

The back of his neck looks so white in the dim light. All I have to do is stab down and this nightmare will be over. He deserves to die in his drunken sleep, for all the times he grabbed me by the ears and slammed my head into the wall. Jack Thompson deserves to be paralyzed from the neck down, to live in a world so helpless, just like I feel.

Then something snaps in me. Some kind of warmth spreads from my toes up into my legs; it floods my stomach like a shot of schnapps and moves to my heart. My grip is released and the knife clatters on the floor.

God's Peace. This is what they call peace. I've never known it before.

I have to get out of here. I can't live like this anymore.

An hour later, a trucker pulls over to pick me up. I'm finally free and heading east, back to where this all started, back to my gang, back to where I belong.

I never see my father alive again.

THERE IS HOPE

For years, I wandered though life with my pain splashing over the edges when I couldn't control it. I self-medicated with liquor and pushed myself towards education and career, anything to keep my mind off all the dark emotion that filled my life.

God had a plan for me, and I thank Him every day that he blessed me with such a wonderful wife. Her goodness and fortitude kept me from falling off the tracks again and again.

I swore that I would never become the abusive person my father was. Even though there was no physical violence, I used silence as a weapon to control and hurt my wife and children. In my workplace, I was loved and respected, but at home, I needed to have all the control so that I could carry on my patterns of abuse, just like my dad.

It was scary one morning to realize that I gave off the same strong alcoholic odours that I remembered from my own childhood. I hated myself for becoming like him. I was walking around carrying a pail that was 98 percent full and ready to splash. If my kids made any noise when I was hung over, I would lash out at them in a negative expression of anger, giving them fear, doubt and worry.

I was lucky to have found Jesus Christ, my Lord and Saviour, when I did or who knows what the next splash would have brought. The new love and grace that He brought into my life changed everything, and I can never go back to being that selfish person who was full of self hatred.

I was still so full of emotion, though, and it frustrated me that Jesus didn't just come along and empty my pail.

Our lives are a journey, and to take the next step, we have to be honest with ourselves about the stored emotion that is inside of us. If Jesus were to just take it all away, then we would learn nothing from our suffering and wouldn't be able to use it to help others into the light.

We have to look at the pails of our own suffering and shame to see what we really are before the healing process can begin.

> *Romans 12:2* - "Do not conform any longer to the pattern of this world, but be transformed by the renewing of your mind. Then you will be able to test and approve what God's will is—His good, pleasing and perfect will."

WHAT IS IN YOUR PAIL? SELF DIAGNOSTICS

Why do you have to look in your pail?

The truth is that if you don't want to look inside at what you've stored emotionally, then eventually it will come out on its own. When it gets full enough, you will splash with negative emotions, and the effects of your darkest secrets will be exposed. You and anyone around you will be drenched in that past shame, and it will only lead to storing more anger in your pail. The saddest part is that you will also be adding to the pails of those you love the most.

I think it is best to not wait for that splash but to look into the murky, oily water to see the negative things that have affected your life. This way, you can purge your feelings in a controlled environment and begin the healing process.

I disagree with concentrating wholly on those nasty experiences in an obsessive way since reliving them may only add more emotional waste to your pail.

I have come up with some categories of questions that might help you or someone you love determine if they have a full pail that results in a destructive anger problem.

Denial is the first major hurdle to overcome. If you are not honest with yourself, then healing and resolution are not possible.

PRAYER FOR SELF DISCOVERY

LORD JESUS,
This is a big step for me. I am going to examine my childhood, my relationships, my behaviours and reactions. I need Your help to properly see things in an unbiased way. Renew my mind. Keep me out of denial of those things that are especially painful and give me the assurance that You are with me and guiding my thoughts and plans.

Help me especially to concentrate first on my own behaviours rather than my spouse, parents or children. I know that my healing is personal and is about me first and foremost. Allow me to know that all others' healing is in Your hands and anything that comes is a blessing. If I become afraid and want to stop, please grant me Your strength to go on, with the hope of healing always there in my mind.

AMEN.

THE PAIL TEST

Personality Traits

Do you or the ones you love possess any of these qualities? If so, the process of dealing with these types of personalities consistently adds negative emotion to your pail.

- *Belligerent Arguing:* This quality develops from the powerful high one gets when proving his or her points through the manipulation of thoughts and ideas. It overrides our sensitivity to other's feelings. Our need to hammer home our own points and to 'win' takes over the desire to come to a mutual understanding.

- *Time Perspectives:* This quality is an obsession with time to the point that only your time is important. For example, one of my clients has time issue; when she is late for an appointment, there is a good excuse, but when anyone else is late and causes her to wait, she loses it. This kind of time obsession can lead to negative stored anger.

- *Constant Comparison:* Society teaches us from childhood that we have to compare ourselves to others and be better than them. You can't just play hockey; you have to be the best on your team or in your league. It's not enough to have a loving wife that cares for you; your wife has to care for you more than anyone else on your radar. Constantly comparing yourself to others or being compared will add to your pail.

- *Intolerance:* Some people cannot understand the ways in which we differ from one another. The root of intolerance is ignorance and fear of the unknown. It produces a need to separate people into groups in order to reduce their humanity. Many times, this kind of profiling is done to gain a feeling of superiority and control over them.

- *Win or Lose Temperament:* Like belligerent arguing, win-lose situations are conflicts that are magnified until they become ultimatums. The potential for loss becomes so great that we become afraid to continue with what we believe is right.

- *The Defensive Attitude:* This irrational way of thinking occurs when we put ourselves in a defensive position even though no offensive action is taking place. Being defensive has its place when someone attacks you without justification. When we are overly sensitive or insecure about our position, then many times we develop this pattern in order to protect ourselves or others unnecessarily.

Frequency and Intensity

- Do you experience frequent angry episodes?
- Do minor events set off fires of anger on a regular basis?
- Do you feel constant tension in your life?
- Do simple requests turn into big fights?
- Do you consider yourself a very intense person?
- Are your reactions not in proportion to the intensity of the action? (For example, a co-worker challenges you with a minor correction and your response is to feel so threatened that you want to physically fight them or quit on the spot.)
- Do you experience anger that lasts for an extended period of time, so much so that it interferes with your work and enjoyment of life?
- Do you relive anger over and over in your head? (Some clients will practice the fight in their head 30 or 40 times before they even get home.)
- Have you ever experienced "black-out" fits of anger where you were conscious but there is no memory of what you have done? (Abusive alcoholics get a blank look in their face or emptiness in their eyes, as if the person you know is no longer present, before exploding in anger.)
- Have you seen or been a part of an experience where the anger is so great that you no longer feel like you are in control of your body but are watching from a distance? (These types of black-out explosions can be a sign of spiritual attack or

psychological breakdown and often cannot be recalled the next day.)

Verbal Abuse

+ Is there, or has there been, sudden and unpredictable screaming, yelling or violence (emotional or physical) in your relationships at home, work or in play?

+ Have you experienced intense verbal outbursts during regular activities? (Road rage is an example of this kind of intense reaction during the daily commute to and from work.)

+ Are threats a regular part of your arguments? ("I want a divorce" is heard far too frequently during inconsequential arguments.)

+ Are ultimatums a part of the response to angry expressions? ("Either you stop being friends with her, or I'm leaving.")

+ Do you turn anger into silence for an extended period of time? (Some Christian couples I counsel haven't had intimate relations for years and yet they refuse to talk about it. That extended silence and lack of intimacy adds so much stored anger to our pails.)

Victimization

+ Have you been a victim of violence used to control?
+ Have you been a victim of assault and battery?
+ Have you been sexually assaulted in any form?

- Have you been witness to destructive acts? (Witnessing or taking part in things, like hitting holes in the wall or people hitting themselves in the chest.)
- Have you been the subject of prolonged or frequent insults?
- Were you or are you bullied, or are you in close proximity to a bully?
- Have you watched someone you love being victimized in a violent way? (Seeing your parents fight adds a tremendous amount of stored anger.)
- Have you experienced intolerance in any form? (This includes not seeing the reality that every person is different and we all process information in a different way, as well dividing people into race, class and religion in prejudice.)

Expectations

- Have you suffered from unrealistic or exceptionally high expectations? (Many kids that have grown up in the church have had high religious expectations put on them that has led to rebellion and stored anger.)
- Have you ever been made to feel inferior by loved ones?
- Do you have expectations of yourself that cannot be met?
- Have you been made to feel like you are not physically attractive?
- Have you been made to feel like you were not smart enough? (Many times, this stored anger comes from

teachers who have made their students feel bad about themselves.)

- Have you consistently been left out, excluded or singled out from a group?

Trust

- Do you suffer from abandonment issues? (Abandonment issues occur when you feel like you've been left without a home or with no one to go to when you need it. My clients describe it like they are standing outside a warm house that they aren't allowed into.)

- Have you been betrayed by loved ones or someone in a position of authority?

- Do you feel like you have no relationship with your parents?

- Have you lost trust in yourself or others in relationships?

- Have you been trying to perform to your parent's standards but have not succeeded in getting their approval?

- Has religion been placed as a priority above your needs to the point where you feel like you can't compete with God? (The most common example of this type of inadequacy is among pastor and missionary kids. Their parents are so focused on their spiritual life that they ignore the pain of their own children. The anger caused by this can lie unresolved for years.)

Shame

- Has self medication become a negative pattern in your life? (Using alcohol or drugs to block out personal failures, shame, frustration or unhappiness with your current situation. This cycle reinforces the negative feelings that it is trying to suppress.)

- Do you feel a strong sense of guilt, embarrassment, unworthiness or disgrace because of something that has happened in your life? (Shame is the internalization of the belief that somehow we are bad.)

- Do you feel like others are shaming you on a regular basis? (Many of these instances are imagined.)

- Do you feel ashamed of past deeds and have extreme feelings of guilt?

- Do you believe that you are defective, inadequate or an evil person because of an action done to you in the past? (Why was I picked to suffer? Why would God do this me?)

Obsessive Thinking

- Do you obsess over everyday worries, doubts and fears?

- Does money turn into a constant argument or obsession in your life? (One of my clients is only happy when the bills are paid at the end of each month. His childhood of poverty has made him overly obsessed with money to the point where he goes through every bank statement with a fine-toothed comb and drills his wife about her every expenditure.)

- Do you easily get upset with time issues? (When someone is late, do you lose your temper and start a fire? Do you wait for people to be late to unload on them?)

- Does every disagreement seem to turn into an argument? (Any challenge to authority leads to an argument that quickly turns emotional. I have a client who will get red faced and overly passionate over any discussion.)

- Does every situation turn into one where you have to either win or lose? (In these situations, there is no sensitivity to the fact that there will not be a winner or loser. People make it so that they have to win at all costs.)

RESULTS OF THE PAIL QUIZ

If you've answered these questions honestly, then you will begin to see the negative emotion that is stored in your pail or the pail of someone close to you.

Since some of the answers to the questions might have a greater intensity for you than others , this is not an exact science for adding up how much stored negative emotion you have in your pail.

The fact is that each individual processes negative experiences in a different way. Some people can bury them so deep they don't remember them, while others let them wash right off. Write down the intensity of each situation that you said yes to, and if you have several intense reactions to those negative experiences, then it is clear that you ready for a splash.

In my original anger management course, I had the attendants write a number between 1-10 depending on the frequency and intensity for each question. For any of the abuse questions, I get them to double or triple that number. At the end of the test, they would add up their numbers to see just how full their pail really was.

If after answering these questions you find that you've said yes frequently, then you are most likely on the brink of a splash. This type of testing is not scientific, but it can be a clear indicator that you might have a serious anger issue. When you tally up exactly how many of these questions you relate to, then you will see that things need to change.

If you are doing this test for a loved one, it can help you to see that they need counselling or outside help to make them realize their anger problem and heal those past wounds.

Exercise - Name Your Losses (Real or Imagined)

Think about each thing you have lost in your life and write them down. Write each loss out and grieve the loss with a special ceremony of your design. You can burn the paper or bury it to show yourself that you have started to let those losses go. Let yourself go through the grieving process and then release those losses from your life.

Trust in the Lord to help you get back what you have lost or to replace it with something new. With each loss, you have to see it and grieve for it appropriately.

> *Joel 2:25* - "I will repay you for the years the locusts have eaten—the great locust and the young locust, the other locusts and the locust swarm—my great army that I sent among you."

PRAYER FOR SURRENDERING ANGER ISSUES TO GOD

LORD JESUS,

Today I surrender to You my need to acknowledge the wounds that are in my life. I acknowledge my need to go through the sanctification process with my anger. I know that You want to sanctify me so that I can be released into the Spirit of Life and be free from the spirit of sin and death.

I surrender to you Jesus, my need to deal with anger. I acknowledge to You that my anger is directing my life in the following areas: in my home life, my work life, my social interactions and my _____.

I accept that healing my anger is a slow process but commit to being open to your direction. You are relentlessly tender and compassionate towards me in spite of my sins and faults. I choose to no longer live as a victim to my anger but choose to trust in Your love for me. Thank You for assuring me that You are with me on the journey to use the gift of self control over my anger issues.

AMEN.

2. WHAT IS ANGER?

The phone keeps ringing and ringing but neither of us want to answer it. We both know who it is on the other end of the line.

"It's your mother, Mark, you answer it!" MaryBelle is still furious about the last time she had to answer the phone. My mother started calling her a string of profanities so bad that my kind wife ended up crying.

She finally picks up the phone as I stare blankly at her, afraid to confront my mother.

"Is this the f**king school teacher? Where is Mark? I don't want to talk to you. Mark is too good for you. He can find someone way prettier than you. You know there are lots of pretty nurses at the hospital where he works."

Her words were slurred, and even before MaryBelle passed me the phone, I knew that she was drunk again and out of control.

A burning rage that had built up inside of me takes hold. There was no way I was going to let my mother who abandoned and betrayed me abuse the woman I loved.

*"Stop calling here. We don't want you in our lives!" I scream
and slam down the phone.*

*It rang again a moment later, but we just unplug the phone
from the wall.*

*The next day, I am at my job in the hospital and I get a page
to come to the emergency room. Standing there, drunk and
swaying on her feet, is my mom. She is mumbling and slurring to
my co-workers, asking where her son is.*

*I feel a deep swell of shame seeing her like that, and I pray
that a hole will open up in the Earth and swallow me. She sees me
and starts to yell at me, calling me horrible names and telling me
that I am a pitiful excuse for a son. I try to reason with her to
make her leave, but it is no use; she is on a rampage.*

*Eventually, the security guards grab her, and I watch as they
escort her out the door. Anger like I've never known burns up
inside of me, and my whole body starts to shake and sweat. This is
so wrong! However, along with the burning anger is the guilt and
fear of closing out the only parent I had left.*

*Yet I know that I have to protect my family and my job. I
have to defend the woman that has stood beside me through all of
my struggles. My anger showed me that I need to stand up and
confront my dark past.*

> Matthew 21:12 – "Jesus entered the temple area and drove
> out all who were buying and selling there. He overturned
> the tables of the money changers and the benches of those
> selling doves."

POSITIVE ANGER – HELPING US SEE THE TRUTH IN THE DARKNESS

Anger in itself is not a bad thing, an evil attribute or a sin. Like all emotions, anger was given to us from God, and when directed in a positive way, it can be a powerful tool to make changes in our hearts, our lives and our world. When you feel angry, it is a clear sign that something is wrong in the situation and needs to be changed.

As we read above, Jesus was furious that his beloved temple was being used to cheat people out of their money. He did not want the sacred place that was his home to be turned into a marketplace where corrupt people could prosper.

When I see corruption in the Church, racism on the streets, pollutions in our waters and greed in our financial system that leaves working people homeless, I feel the flame of indignation rise up in me to do something to change the injustices in this world.

This kind of mental anger can be used to motivate social change and to prevent further injustices that are all too frequent in our world. Does child abuse, the torture of innocent people, children dying of poverty and the genocide of millions infuriate you?

It should. God wants us to focus that anger into figuring out ways to stop the horrors of inequality and barbarism that still remain. That collective and peaceful expression of anger is the force needed to help start the movement against the evils of racism and discrimination in non-violent ways.

On a more personal level, I feel anger when someone is trying to hurt me or my family. I get angry when others are emotionally controlling me. I suddenly feel a fire light up inside me that makes me want to act out in a strong movement of change.

Anger is a gift from God to show us **something is wrong.** Anger is a God-given gift that helps us live our lives in the right way. This flame is the canary in the coal mine that feels the noxious gases first. It keeps the wolves at bay and lights up our path so we do not stumble into the ways of evil men.

For most of us, the biggest benefit of positively expressed anger is that it is **a powerful sign that it is time to set boundaries.**

PRAYER FOR ACCEPTING RIGHTEOUS ANGER

LORD JESUS,
Thank you for giving us an example of righteous anger and for showing me that anger is an emotion that can be present in all of us as human beings. I know, however, that my anger is not always righteous. Help me to identify when I step over the line from positive anger to negative anger that hurts people. I pray for wisdom and power to change those things in my world that need to be changed for the better and to use righteous anger in a positive way. Help me to identify and set boundaries to protect myself and my emotions. Teach me through the following lessons, Lord, to express my anger in a way that is pleasing to You and not destructive to me and my loved ones.

AMEN.

SETTING BOUNDARIES

A boundary is a psychological or mental line in the sand that you do not want crossed. A boundary is used to protect your emotions, your rights and your freedoms as a human being. Having boundaries allows you to see when people are trying to control you, take away your freedom or cause you emotional or physical pain.

A good use of anger is that it shines a light on **abnormal behaviours** or actions that aren't acceptable in relationships. In these key moments, it is essential to resist expressing negative anger and out-of-control flames of yelling, hitting or silence. In this book, you will learn ways to realize these moments as indicators that someone has crossed your boundaries. They have trespassed into unhealthy actions that have to be stopped and patterns that must be broken.

In the moments when our rights are infringed upon, the fires of anger make us realize that we have to stand up for ourselves and become assertive. In **Matthew 10:16** Jesus says, "I am sending you out like sheep among wolves. Therefore be as shrewd as snakes and as innocent as doves." He knew we were going out in the world and told us that we needed to stand up so that we could be as smart and firm as he was.

Being assertive is how we respond with gentle firmness when people cross our boundaries. It's within the assertive model where we can find the true benefits of positive anger. We must find the equilibrium in our communication. It is the balance where you are not taking any damage while not inflicting damage in retaliation either.

Emotions in themselves are neither right nor wrong. How these emotions are expressed is the way to determine if they are negative or positive in yourselves and others.

Sometimes it is obvious. If you are being physically attacked, anger gives you that extra fire to defend yourself and your family. It triggers the adrenaline that makes you strong physically and mentally when your physical safety is threatened. That super-human strength can resolve a dangerous situation.

As a former school counsellor, I offered a preventative program to protect children from being sexually abused. If children are taught to say no using their anger in a positive way, the abusers will often stop. That sudden flare up of strong emotion, even in one so young, can keep a predator at bay.

The mental strength that anger gives us can also be a very powerful tool. Mentally, anger can make us stubborn and compel us to continue on in the face of great danger or social injustice. This is very useful when people are trying to intimidate us to take away our freedoms and rights. Emotional stress can be debilitating, but when there is something more important at stake, we can use that anger to our advantage.

One of the most common issues in lives that are dominated by anger is the fact that people light their own fires. Anger is a God-given gift to show us that something is wrong in our present situation.

When a splash takes place and is lit by the fire of anger, there is a temporary release of the stored emotion before the pail is filled again. That momentary release is like a teapot blowing off steam. The pressure is gone but the water is still boiling underneath. This release turns into an integral part of the lives of those dominated by anger. It becomes a seemingly necessary function for them to feel "normal."

So we start our own fires. We make up things that are wrong so we can have a reason to splash and ignite into angry explosions. The boundaries crossed are imaginary. The violations are only perceived that way.

Lighting your own fire is one of the most common problems among people with serious anger issues. They become addicted to the problem and the release of emotion. These people appear to need "drama" and therefore go out of their way to create it when the opportunity arises.

When the warning fire of anger is combined with a splash of emotion from our already full pails, there is sure to be a release of negative anger.

From the diagnostic test, you can see just how full your pail really is. Personally, my pail had been full for decades, and until I learned to empty it, there was always the chance of a splash. Most of the emotion inside the pail is negative anger that has been suppressed and will explode once released in a splash.

WHAT IS A SPLASH?

In my definition, a splash is a sudden release of stored emotion. Emotions run through us like liquids, and if we cannot process them, then they fill our pails. From past psychological injuries to everyday frustrations, we add to our pail all the time. Our pails can get pretty full, and all of that liquid emotion is not only toxic but erodes our relationships like acid erodes metal. Much of the stored emotion can become flammable like water that has gasoline or oil polluting it.

Then something knocks us off balance. With that pail perched precariously on our head, it's hard enough to just walk around—never mind doing anything that requires quick action!—without spilling.

Exercise – Expectation Breathing

The first thing to realize is that much of our anger comes from unfulfilled expectations, especially the anger we fill up with when things in our everyday lives don't go right.

Imagine that your expectations are a cloud around your head. There is nowhere to run and trying to think it away is just getting you more frustrated. The only way get rid of it is to embrace those expectations fully, let them spread through your body and become you.

Take a deep breath in, count to four if you need to regulate how deep it should be. While you are breathing in, imagine all of those expectations entering into you and becoming you until you are full of them.

Breathe out and let them go. Feel the expectations drain out of you with your exhalation. By becoming you, those expectations have changed from volatile gas to normal air. Keep breathing out until every last bit of that expectation is gone from your body.

For the rest of the book, I will use the word "trigger" to denote any action, word or feeling that throws a person off balance. It could be a name someone calls you or a duty somebody forgets that "triggers" you off balance. Once triggered, you are no longer calm and assertive like someone who is balanced but are jerking all over the place emotionally.

With a pail full of toxic and dangerous emotions, some of them are bound to splash out into the immediate area. That sudden loss of control over our emotions can result in things like crying, insomnia or compulsive actions. We've all lost control at some point in our lives by breaking down in a situation where we feel we have no control over what will happen next.

Yet when the fire of anger is in front of us imploring that something needs to be changed, any sudden splash can quickly become an explosion and an out-of-control fire.

For some of us, the negative emotions that we store are flammable, and when they touch the revealing torch of anger, it becomes an explosion that leads to abuse.

These negative expressions of anger can happen in our own minds, with our partners, in our families, in the community, in our work places and in the church.

Once a splash is ignited, there is almost always another splash from those who are directly involved. Ignited splashes happen inside our hearts, inside of our minds and outside of us to create a wall of silence; they burn other people directly with violence, and splashes can burn out whole relationships.

Splashes that are lit up into negative expressions of anger lead to aggressive abuse, passive aggressive abuse, psychological abuse, internalized shame, guilt, and even physical disease and illness. Later, I will look closely into the different types of negative expressions that lead to abuse and sickness.

The first thing is learning to recognize the warning signs of a potential splash. Some warning signs may include tension in the neck, chest, forehead and back. Sometimes, we clench our jaws or break out in a sweat when we are about to lose our tempers. One of my clients even starts to twitch right before he splashes over and ignites in negative anger.

Exercise – Changing Perspectives

When you feel that you are about to splash over with negative anger, one of the best things you can do is change your perspective.

The easiest way to do this is to leave the environment that you are in and take a walk. Your legs are moving and the blood that was clotting your judgment is forced to pass through the rest of your body. Even nature itself will give you a different outlook on what is really happening inside of you.

If you cannot leave the situation, then try to change your perspective mentally. If you cannot fathom the perspectives of the other people involved in the potential conflict, then imagine the perspective of a fly on the wall or some other random person.

Getting out of your own head for just a moment is enough to stabilize the shifting pail and regain balance.

Step outside of yourself and find the equilibrium that you need to go on without a splash.

An emotional warning sign might be when you start to feel like someone has done an injustice towards you: "It's just not fair." You repeat the injustice over and over, working yourself into a frenzy. All of the buried feelings of neglect, abandonment or inadequacy might rise to the surface of your consciousness.

Personally, I can tell that my pail is filling up when I can't sleep. I start to watch too much television and crave the old habits of escape into intoxication. I feel like I need to make everything perfect and am immediately frustrated that it won't be. I know I'll have a splash when I feel like things are going too fast and are not in my control. In my emotional world, I can't process that instability. I become very conscious of people shaming me or making me feel bad about myself. All of those things are warning signs that I'm about to blow.

The other common issue that makes people splash is when they are triggered. A trigger is like a match that will always light a fire. Once the trigger is pulled, you are locked into an escalation that will not stop until there is a splash and both of you get burned.

LIGHTING YOUR OWN FIRES

When someone with a full pail splashes over the edge and lights up that negative emotion with the fire of anger, there is an immediate release of pressure.

It is similar to a natural gas well that needs to be burned off. Without the occasional release, there can be a deadly explosion. People with anger issues get addicted to that release of pressure, when they splash out and become angry in a negative way.

Many times, there is nothing to be angry about; there is no fire lit to show that things have gone awry and the only burning fire is an internal one. The anger addict then creates a situation in which something is wrong so he can feel justified in splashing and burning those around him.

They might pick on someone's qualities that annoy them or bring up past issues just to fight and release some of that stored emotion.

> *Isaiah 50:10-11* – "Who among you fears the LORD and obeys the word of his servant? Let him who walks in the dark, who has no light, trust in the name of the LORD and rely on his God. But now, all you who light fires and provide yourselves with flaming torches, go, walk in the light of your fires and of the torches you have set ablaze. This is what you shall receive from my hand: You will lie down in torment."

Heed the Word of God when it comes to lighting your own fire, for those who do will lie down in torment. Creating anger where there is no need for it will leave you alone, and the experience will fill your pail right back up as well as filling the pails of everyone around you.

PRAYER FOR LIGHTING YOUR OWN FIRE

LORD JESUS,
I have come to realize that I am guilty of lighting my own fires rather than seeking You and walking in Your light. I regularly get angry at others, often for no reason, and I let my anger splash out and hurt others. Help me to recognize what I am doing, creating anger when there is no need for it, justifying my actions to myself and giving myself that 'fix' of anger that somehow releases the pressure building up in me. I pray for insight that I may not light my own fires of anger, hurting myself and those with whom I come into contact.
AMEN.

3. ESCALATION – THE AUTOMATIC STAIRWAY TO DESTRUCTION

"No." The response came out of my mouth before she even finished proposing it. Just the thought of sinking money into a toy store set off my irrational fears of getting in over our heads financially. There was no way this would ever make money, and I couldn't understand why she would want to spend her time in a proposition that wouldn't be financially successful.

"You're just like my dad!" MaryBelle stands up, her face red and her hands shaking. "Everything my mom ever tried to do in her life, he just shot down and never even gave her a chance."

We had just bought a house and now she wants to quit her teaching job for this new risky venture with her family. I can't believe we are even having this discussion.

She knows I hate it when she says that about her father. I can feel my blood boil when she compares me to her father. I know that she always resented her dad for holding her mother back creatively. The last person I saw myself as in the world was her father.

"I am not like him in the least. Stop making me the bad guy around here. Why do you even want to do this anyways? You'll never make a dime off of this. Your family is always trying to use us to get what they want. I am always playing second fiddle to them."

I can see that she is crying now, angrier by the second. "You always put my ideas down without ever listening to them or caring about what makes me happy. You just don't trust me!"

"I don't care if you want work in this little project of yours, but when it comes to putting big bucks behind it, then forget it. We can barely make our payments as it is."

"Why do you always think that I'm trying to put us in the poor house? Why don't you ever trust me that I know what I'm talking about?"

She walks away from me to the other room, just needing some space. I am not done with her, though. This is far from over.

"I do trust you! It's just that I'm going to be the only one making money around here. It's all on my shoulders. You don't understand how hard I work. You never give me credit for all the stress that I'm under. You'll never be able to do it all. You barely have the time to get stuff done around the house as it is now!"

"Oh, poor you! I just hate that you never give me credit for all that I do around here. You only think about yourself. I'm so sick of you complaining about how hard your life is," MaryBelle screams at me from the doorway.

"I should have never married you in the first place! You've done nothing but hurt my chances at being successful! Then you just turn it around and make me look like the bad guy!"

"Well, maybe we should get a divorce then!" She slams the door in my face.

My fists and jaws are clenched. I want to go after her and shake some sense into her.

Like a wall of flame springing up from the earth, my world turns to silence. I retreat deep into myself where she can no longer hurt me. I turn on the TV, raising the volume until I can no longer hear the screaming in my head.

It will be days until we speak again.

WHAT IS THE ESCALATOR OF ANGER?

Most people don't have instant splashes or flare outs in which they lose control without any warning signs. For the most part, angry people need something to trigger them so that they step onto what I've coined the **Escalator of Anger.**

Why do I think of it as an escalator? It is similar to a stairway in the fact that, with each successive phase, your temper gets higher; but the reason it's called an escalator is because once you get on it, you are automatically headed to the top without even trying.

The crazy part is that when we do get on the escalator, we can't see that it ends in a cliff that drops us right into our full pail. The explosion that follows is always ugly and regularly ends in abuse. If you've ever tried to run down an upward-moving escalator, you know that it is very hard to come back down once you are on.

I hope that by explaining the phases, you will be able to jump off the escalator before it's too late. The hope that God gives to us is that we can gain control of our anger, and when that happens, we can take charge of the escalation.

PHASE 1 – THE TRIGGER

A trigger is the release mechanism for a gun that, once pulled, sets the bullet in motion. Triggers are made so that they are accessible and easy to pull. Once they are pulled, there is no going back.

Our personal triggers are the things that we are most sensitive about. These are the areas in our minds and our relationships that are the most volatile. It could be a rejection, perceived rejection, slight, insult, or a certain condescending or patronizing tone. The trigger could be the reminder of when trust was broken. If someone ignores or dismisses us, it can trigger off our anger. Sometimes a trigger can even be a single word like "flirt" that puts us on the escalator of anger.

For me, the trigger was being referred to as being "just like my dad." I was insecure about repeating the mistakes of both of our fathers and didn't want to be compared to them. For my wife, her trigger was my instant refusal to listen to her ideas.

To get onto the escalator of anger, there needs to be two people involved. As soon as one person is triggered, they will immediately try to trigger the other.

Think about all the times you've gotten into fights with your significant other. As soon as they get angry, they start saying things just to make you mad. They have been triggered and want you to join them on the path to crisis.

The intense anger that is flaming through our minds when we are triggered burns all rational thought away. We need to validate our intense anger and begin using words like never, awful, terrible or unacceptable, to raise the stakes of the struggle that is about to ensue.

Suggested Reactions:

When dealing with our own triggers, we have to realize that they always have to do with our self-esteem. Being called stupid doesn't bother us if we are secure in our intelligence. If we are worried about our weight, however, being called fat can make us enraged and ready to fight.

When someone has been triggered around you, what can you do?

Trigger Exercise

What are your triggers? Can you list them? Can you sit down with a pen and paper and think of all the words, thoughts and ideas that make you so mad you can no longer think?

Sit down with a blank piece of paper and think of all the things that really make you angry. It might help to think of past or current fights you are having and remember what it was that initially set you off. Look at them to see what you think is the truth or what you are just insecure about.

What you may find is that the triggers are just false perceptions that you have come to believe as truth. If it is something that you are truly insecure about, then it is time to start making changes in your life to alter those insecurities.

If you know your triggers beforehand then it will be easy to recognize them and stay off the escalator.

You can tell immediately when the other person has been triggered by their change in body language and tone. That is the moment to either change the subject or get the hell out of there. Go to the bathroom, the other room or for a walk.

To escape the trigger, you have to take away its power by realizing that it is not the truth. What someone says, their tone, the words or inflection cannot put you into a box. You are in control of who you are, your actions and what you believe about yourself.

The best solution is to realize the trigger, reaffirm that you didn't mean it personally and tell them that you are sorry for saying it. Let them know that it is not really true and help them regain control over their perspective. Get on their side and stay off the escalator!

Phase 2 – Adding Fuel to the Fire

If we don't realize that we have been triggered, then we will wade into the fray with both guns drawn. We truly believe that we have been deeply insulted and wronged. We want to build momentum in our anger and do so by repeating negative phrases in our head, something I call "negative self-talk."

For instance, during the argument with my wife, I started adding fuel to the fire by insulting her family and insinuating negative things about them. My wife continued to add fuel to the fire by using words like "never" and "not trusting me." These fed into our insecurities and set us off balance so that our pails splashed out with negative expressions of anger.

Suggested Reactions:

If you see yourself starting to add fuel to the fire, insulting and baiting the other person, then you have to do something quickly before they are thrown off balance and splash. Leave the room until you are in control of your emotions and then apologize. Being vulnerable about your sensitivity almost always diffuses the situation.

However, this is easier said than done. It is very difficult to be humble about our own sensitivity. If you want to truly manage your anger, then you have to admit to yourself and the other person that sometimes you are not in control. This will help you get back your control.

If it is someone else that has been triggered and is now adding fuel to the fire, then you have to turn off your sensitivity. I like to think of it as a sailboat in a harbour. When someone is triggered, it is like a storm suddenly blows in from the sea. Don't get sucked into reacting and **KEEP YOUR SAILS DOWN**. If you remove your own sensitivity, then you cannot be blown around by their anger or their baiting. You will not be thrown off balance and will not splash with your own pail.

If they do not calm down with you using your own relaxed energy, then you should try to tell them in a way that isn't condescending that "I am sensitive to how you feel right now, but I know that this isn't the time to fix things. Let's give it a couple of hours and we'll talk."

Give a sincere apology for having triggered them. If you don't feel like you've done anything wrong, then say, "I am sorry that what I said made you angry; I didn't mean it like that."

Sometimes, we are both desperate to keep the fight alive because there is so much stored anger and we unconsciously know that this fight will be a release. It is a way to start our own fires while getting back at those that hurt us.

PHASE 3 – FIGHT OR FLIGHT

This is the stage where we lose control of normal communication. Adrenaline is coursing through our bodies. We are both thrown off balance and consumed by our emotions. Our pails splash out onto each other with devastating effects.

MaryBelle wanted to flee when she recognized that the situation was out of control. I followed her to the door, and she had to turn and fight. It is the same instinctual reaction we have when we are physically attacked.

At this point on the escalator of anger, both parties don't even realize what's happening. They just want to hurt each other so that their own pain can stop. They falsely believe that, by attacking, they can beat the other into submission. Instead, the fight only intensifies.

There can be no winner on the escalator of anger — everybody on it loses.

Suggested Reactions:

At this point, it is nearly impossible to resist the physicality of the rage that is burning between you. The chemical reactions going on inside are in control, not your mind.

If you can pull yourself away, then do it. Lock yourself in a bathroom and stick your fingers in your ears until the other person stops yelling.

If you cannot get out of the room, then sit down and start to breathe deeply. Remain silent to the other person's insults and refuse to continue the engagement of anger. If you are worried about being physically attacked, then do not break eye contact.

Sometimes having one person become totally still can make the other even angrier and push them into the next critical phase. Usually, they will become frustrated with your silence and leave the room.

My wife tries to do something productive until the adrenaline has left her system. Cleaning out the garage or taking a walk are good ways to regain your balance. Remember to allow yourself plenty of time to cool down before resuming communication. Putting on your favourite music will also help to stop the negative self-talk that will ensue.

PHASE 4 – THE CRISIS AND THE SPLASH

You know that you have reached the crisis stage when the consequences of your actions go beyond the fight. Most of the time, the crisis and splash phase ends with verbal abuse, usually on both sides. There is crying, hurt feelings and resentment. Dire threats may be tossed out without thinking about their true cost to the relationship. There might even be physical violence, abuse or the use of silence to control the situation.

It is surprising how quickly a small incident can turn into violence when triggers knock us off balance and our full pails splash into our lives.

It is important to note that both parties are responsible for getting on the escalator of anger. This equalizes the power relationship between the two.

In many of the cases that come through my doors, the physical power is held by the man. He will lash out with physical violence, and because of his strength, he will batter the woman down.

In the next section, we will talk about the cycle of abuse and how this pattern can keep repeating itself over and over.

Suggested Reactions:

Get out. It's that easy. When you see the blank look in the other's eyes that signals violence, whether that violence be emotional, verbal or physical, you need to remove yourself from its reach.

If you are in this situation and you feel any kind of impulse to hurt the other person, then you must realize that you still have a choice. Violence in all of its forms is inexcusable. There is never justification for hitting, screaming down or destroying someone's self-esteem.

Think! Just use your brain in that instance and think. This person loves you, and you love them. They are not an object. You don't hate them. You are just caught on the escalator of anger and this is your last chance to bail.

Exercise – Vent your anger

This requires that you unload your pent up anger on an inanimate object. The process will give you physical and emotional release. Use an empty chair to yell your frustrations at or use a punching bag or pillow to release physical frustrations. Go to a private space and yell, scream, play angry music or vent frustrations verbally in the mirror. Get the splash out of your system before it gets you and your family!

PHASE 5 – BOTTOMING OUT: CRASHING AND SINKING

This is the stage where we come back to reality and realize what we've done. Our senses and logic return. We feel remorse for what we've said and are deeply hurt by what's been said to us. Depression ensues.

In this moment, our heart rate slips below normal and we are both wracked with feelings of shame, depression, sadness and even suicide. It is like we just ran a marathon and cannot go on. Rational thought returns with the exhaustion and so does the regret.

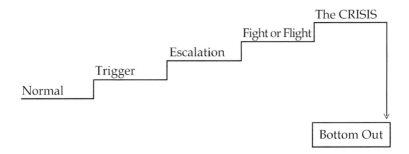

Suggested Reactions:

This is the time you both need to realize that you need help for your anger issues. If you are the one that has just been abused, try not to be cruel but insist that things cannot go on like this. There has to be a change in both the way you deal with your anger and the way that it is expressed. Both sides at this point are open to talking and can see how their anger issue has drained them and others.

Exercise – Write it All Down

Try writing down your feelings in a letter to the person you are angry with and then wait two days and read it again. Ask yourself what your motives are. How would you feel if you received this letter? Writing it down can make you see the scope of the issue, but I warn you **DO NOT email or Facebook the angry letter!** Sending out angry letters will only bring more conflict into your life. Instead, start a diary to help you release pent-up anger and understand your emotions with stories, personal journaling or poetry.

2 Corinthians 10:5 – "We demolish arguments and every pretension that sets itself up against the knowledge of God, and we take captive every thought to make it obedient to Christ."

Proverbs 15:1 – "A gentle answer turns away wrath, but a harsh word stirs up anger."

PRAYER FOR RECOGNIZING TRIGGERS

LORD JESUS,

As I think about how my anger is triggered and words that set me off in anger, I seek your Spirit to help me take every thought and word captive to You. Help me to take the time to think and then pray and give the offensive word to You to hold captive so that I will not be triggered. By Your love for me, let me see that it is just a word, a word that has no power over me. Allow me the strength to stand back and breathe and have self-control. Lord, I also ask that You soften my heart so that I hold back from firing out those trigger words that I know will damage the self-esteem of those I am dealing with.

I pray that You will give me the picture of the escalator and give me the strength to not step onto it by adding fuel to the fire of anger. Help me to keep my sails down and to not react, to stay calm with a peace that passes understanding. Lord, if things start getting out of control, give me the wisdom and strength to walk away for awhile, and to not be physical in my anger. I pray that You would put Your love in my heart for others, pushing out the anger and hatred I feel at that moment. You are strong, give me Your strength. I hold this verse to be true for myself: **Philippians 4:13** – "I can do all things through Christ who strengthens me."

AMEN.

4. NEGATIVE PATTERNS IN COMMUNICATION

My wife looks at me expectantly with the pregnancy test results in her hand. A feeling of dread washes over me.

"I told you that I didn't want children!" I yell before she can even start explaining what she is doing. "I thought you were on birth control."

I can see the tears well up in her eyes, but I go on regardless.

"That was one of the rules I made when I we got engaged: NO CHILDREN. I don't want to screw up any little kids the way my dad screwed me up. You knew that, and you went off birth control anyways. That's so selfish of you!"

I cannot control myself. I know deep down that this negative overreaction is exactly the thing she doesn't need right now. What kind of a person am I to react this way?

The old voice of inner condemnation rises up in me: You are an idiot, Mark. You have a chance to have a family, but you are such a worthless person that you are going to ruin them all. How do you expect to provide for them? You are poor in every way and will always be poor.

Shut UP! I scream inside my head and open my eyes to see my wife's expectant face.

Suddenly, a new glimmer of hope rises inside of me. Maybe things can be different this time. Maybe I'll be able to break all those bad patterns that I've been living in for so long.

Maybe this is my chance to show myself that I can change.

Everyone has fallen into some negative habits about the way we communicate with ourselves and with the ones we love. These patterns have to do with the way we talk, act and treat each other in our daily lives. If we can spot these patterns, then it is easy to reduce our anger and the splashes that come from it almost immediately. Look at your own way of communicating to see if you fall into these patterns.

ULTIMATUMS

An ultimatum occurs when we give or are being given a choice between two options with severe consequences. Ultimatums are usually given when the angry person feels powerless and wants to control the situation.

Angry ultimatums are a common pattern that evolves from stored anger. I will not tolerate this behaviour. If you don't stop seeing your friend then I will…

If you recognize that you are giving ultimatums, then you need to realize that an ultimatum almost always provokes the unwanted behaviour and backfires. Trying to control someone's behaviour through ultimatums usually leads to more fighting, separation and the escalation of emotions.

If someone is giving you ultimatums, it is best to ignore the choice and choose a third option: **I choose neither**. This takes away the power of the ultimatum.

OVERREACTION

This occurs when we make things out to be much bigger than they are. We take the current situation and exaggerate its importance, adding trigger words that escalate the situation until it is important enough to justify our anger.

When the severity of the offense is inflated, it makes us champions of lost causes. We then lose perspective in the conflict and act as if a great injustice has taken place.

If you recognize that you overreact, it is best to take a step back from the situation or to look at it from another person's point of view to gain perspective. **Avoid using absolutes and words such as "never," "should" and "always" within the conflict**. Once we learn to recognize that the severity of our anger is from other previous wrongs against us, we can redirect our emotions away from the situation in the moment.

If you are on the receiving end of someone that overreacts, then take a step back from the conflict until the moment of anger has passed. Then point out that the situation is not as severe as it is being portrayed.

SUBJECTIVE RULE MAKING

I had made a rule about children that was purely subjective and used it to control my wife when she wanted to get married. Later, when her maternal instincts kicked in, she didn't want to live by that rule anymore.

Who made that rule? Who makes these rules of "I cannot love you unless you do this and that"? This pattern of making up rules to put someone in the wrong when expectations have not been met is a very subtle negative pattern of irrational thinking.

So many people have arbitrary rules about love.

"If she loved me, then she might help me with the farm more." Or "This woman is mine and I own her."

Who made the rule that you own someone once you get married?

One of my clients made an arbitrary rule that his wife could not deny him sex whenever he wanted it. He claimed that the Bible said that a woman should always obey her husband. He manipulated God's word so that he could get what he wanted.

These kinds of manipulations and subjective rules must be recognized for what they are and challenged in a calm way. When we limit each other with such trivial and irrational regulations, we only cause deep-seated resentment.

GETTING ON THE SAME PAGE

In my counselling experience, many couples get into fights but are not on the same page, making it impossible to come to a resolution. There are two levels of communication: the **emotional page** (when we are focused on personal feelings) and the **logical page** (rational understanding of what is reasonable, correct or incorrect).

In my situation, I was on an emotional page and was dealing with my own insecurities about being a father. My wife, on the other hand, was on a logical page, trying to deal with the situation of our unexpected pregnancy. She could not realize in that moment that my reaction did not have to do with her personally but with my own pail, full of negative emotions about parenting.

The solution was to realize that we were not dealing with the reality of the situation but with my own emotional issues and fear. My wife had to look past the accusations and into the murky waters of my past to realize what was really going on. By leaving her logic and using emotional intelligence, she could have diffused the situation. What I really needed was affirmation that I was not my father.

This may sound easy, but it's really hard to do. We want to get into a fight and defend ourselves when really we just need to listen and then show affection and understanding. When one person confronts the other with emotions, it is very difficult not to be triggered onto the escalator of anger.

As a side note, sometimes when people make comments or observations, they are not being personal. They are on the logical page. If you take those comments emotionally, they become much worse than they were ever intended to be.

When conflict arises, it is imperative to be on the same page. Is this about a logical process of wrongdoing, or is it about feelings and emotions? When you can answer that question, you are well on your way to making peace with each other.

Exercise – Reframing

How many times has someone said something to you and you thought about it for days afterwards? Do you realize that most of the time the person didn't even know what they were saying or that it would hurt you?

Peoples' behaviour can be an indication of where they are with God. Sometimes, the people that are the rudest and hurt you the most are doing so because they haven't realized in their own lives the grace of Jesus and the kindness that He commands in us. Or maybe they just aren't very sensitive.

When someone hurts me, I do not take it personally but use it as a message from God to remember that I, too, may have unintentionally hurt someone in the past.

For every insult received, go out and encourage or compliment someone else. You will find that the sting of whatever hurt you will disappear with the smile you put on someone else's face.

PROCESSING GAPS

My wife processes her intellectual thoughts a lot faster than I do (which has been a blow to my pride). She will look at a situation and, within moments, decide what she wants to do and what the right thing is for her. She'll come to me with her conclusions, and I'll often agree or disagree too quickly because I don't truly understand what's going on.

When I finally catch up, I realize that that I didn't understand the whole situation and now my opinion has changed. I'll go to her with my new outlook, and she is confused and angry, believing that I'm always changing my mind.

The fact is that I haven't really changed my mind; I was just slow getting there. It was not that I didn't have integrity with my decisions; I just didn't have the completed picture to look at. Different processing speeds have nothing to do with integrity.

There is a concept called EQ, or emotional intelligence, which pertains to **one's ability to read** the emotions of ourselves and others. Some of us know how we feel about a situation in the moment, while others cannot define or analyze how they are feeling in the same way. The processing gap in these situations has to do with emotional awareness.

Recognizing this pattern can solve so many problems. Once we know that people need more time to process complicated issues, we can give them the time they need to catch up. Having different processing speeds is not a bad thing; we all have different kinds of intelligence in this life. We have to understand our strengths and weaknesses in order to achieve the equilibrium that we seek.

NEGATIVE SELF-TALK

Negative self-talk is like putting a song on repeat and listening to it until every word is known by heart. When we are trying to learn something, studies have shown that if we repeat it 21 times in a row, then it will stick.

The same is true when we want to believe something negative. If we repeat it enough times, then it becomes truth instead of perspective or opinion.

Have you ever found yourself replaying an offence over and over in your mind until it becomes fact? Worse yet, over time we add past and future offences to the situation until it doesn't even resemble the original offence. If I tell myself 21 times a day that I'm not good enough, then by the end of the day, I truly believe it. There is a compounding and multiplying effect that happens as negative self-talk continues.

Imagine that each issue in our life is like a pen that we are writing with. To resolve that issue, we must write with that pen until the story of the conflict is resolved. When we have constant negative self-talk, we add issues on top of each other until we have a handful of pens.

Have you ever tried to write with a handful of pens? How can we write out our true concerns when we keep adding more pens of offence to write with? Our issues will become crossed over, complicated and the truth of the resolution will never be clear.

To break the cycle of negative self-talk, we must first realize that it's happening. Look at what you are thinking and separate the issues until you are analyzing one single issue. **Write with one pen at a time.**

Once we see our thoughts for what they are, then we can counteract them. The next step is to flip the pattern on its head and begin to use positive self-talk instead. Repeat the positive message to yourself until it starts to sink in.

This life is precious, so why waste it creating negative self-loathing when we can create a positive self-image instead?

THE USE OF SILENCE TO CONTROL

Generational sins are patterns that children learn and repeat in their own families. My parents were violent people, and when I got married, my own pail was very full. Unlike my father, I am a gentle person who abhors the thought of hitting another, even when I am very angry.

When my pail splashes, it forms a wall of fire around me that blocks out those who love me. This wall of silence cannot be penetrated by words, touch, feelings or trust. I use my silence as a way to stop time so that our relationship is on pause until I am ready to continue living a life of regular communication again.

Usually people call this "the silent treatment," and they use it to control the people around them. I use the term **time stopping** with my clients as it speaks to the control issues that this silence stems from.

While in time-stopping mode, we give minimal answers to questions. There is an aura of disappointment in those with whom we are silent. Everyone in the immediate family knows what is happening and all are powerless to do anything about it. Suddenly, the time stopper will get a phone call and break into the friendliest conversation, laughing and joking with the person outside of the family, but after they hang up the phone, the silence continues.

This kind of reaction is the dark side of the time stopping. We have removed the threat of an explosion, but the cold that we leave can be just as damaging. Soon, a time stopper will learn that they can use their silence to control and punish the people around them. The rest of the family will have cooled off and want to return to a normal state of affairs. The accusatory silence that persists is deafening.

Members of the family might even be triggered by our silence and be unbalanced enough to have their own splash.

Then one day, the time stopper starts to communicate again like nothing happened. They are, in fact, often unaware that they finally came to the decision to start talking again. This inconsistency breeds anger and resentment in the rest of the family that can last for years, filling their pails with bitterness.

This pattern can touch all parts of our lives. One time, I was even mad at my dog, Nico, for nipping at me when I touched his food. Instead of outwardly expressing my anger, I stopped time with him, not paying attention to him for two whole days. On the third day when I climbed into my bed, I realized that he had peed all over my pillow. Nico didn't touch my wife's side at all. Every drop of urine was reserved for me! Even dogs will splash out when given the silent treatment.

To start, the goal should be to decrease both the frequency and the impact of time stopping on others and ourselves. Just the realization that this is a harmful expression of anger can vastly reduce its frequency and intensity. One week of silence can be reduced into a two-hour timeout.

Exercise – Helping the Time Stopper

1. **Identify the Behaviour** – We, as the family or friends of the time stopper, have to acknowledge that this is their pattern, and by keeping silent about it, we give it power. The family members all need to be educated so that they can resolve the issue of starting time and decrease the frequency and the impact of time stopping

2. **Mutual Timeout** – The next step is to call for a mutual timeout. Once the negative expression of silence is recognized, both sides should stop communication in order to mirror the effects. Agree to an exact time to resume communication. When you do start communicating again, pick a neutral topic to talk about, one that neither side is overly sensitive about. Once the bond of normal communication is restored, it will be more difficult for the time stopper to fall back into silence.

3. **Get on the Same Page** – The key at this point is to turn the page from emotional reacting to logical reasoning. The issue that caused time to stop should be discussed in an impersonal and logical way to distance sensitive feelings that might lead into more time stopping.

4. **Communication, Not Condemnation** – If there is no condemnation, we will feel that we have the freedom to make profound change. If a person doesn't feel like they are stuck in the role of a "bad" or "evil" person, then they will want to wipe the slate clean and start again. There is a chance that the "non-angry" person will become resentful when they start to feel like they are doing all the work to start time again. We have to treat this like an illness, like diabetes or cancer. Becoming angry at the person that is sick is never good for communal health. As hard as it is, we are taught to be servants to each other like Jesus was a servant to us. The more you talk to each other to work through issues, the more the time stopper will want to talk in the future. Success breeds success, and if you water the plant of communication, it will grow and flower.

5. **The Power of Hugging** – For some, it is difficult to express their love through touch, but in conquering silence and all forms of anger, we should be open to change our standards of personal space. Start off by being in the same room sitting close to each other and progress from there. Hugging can be awkward at first, so you can start by shaking hands or putting an arm around each other. Touching shares the power of our energy and is a powerful healing agent.

PRAYER FOR HEALING "STOPPING TIME"

LORD JESUS,
Please forgive me for my angry reaction to most things in my relationships, especially when I resort to silence. Show me, Lord, another, better way to deal with my anger and my hurt feelings other than shutting others out. I realize that this is the way I use to control and manipulate my family so that I can deal with things at my own speed and time. I want to change and put to death all of those habits I have learned in my life, and I want to learn how to react when things don't go my way. Reveal to me how I hurt others with my silence so that I can see the damage I inflict by my selfish behaviour. Lord, provide me with healthy alternatives to silence when I feel overwhelmed with anger.

AMEN.

Ephesians 4:26, 31-32 – "In your anger, do not sin: do not let the sun go down while you are still angry...Get rid of all bitterness, rage and anger, brawling and slander, along with every form of malice. Be kind and compassionate to one another, forgiving each other, just as in Christ God forgave you."

GOOD COMMUNICATION – MOVING TOWARDS A BETTER LIFE

When people are expressing their anger in a negative way, whether it be with aggression or aggressive silence, only a very small percentage of what the angry person is hearing actually sinks in.

In the moment of the splash with an angry person, we must remember that no matter how eloquent our words are, nothing is getting through. Even worse, they will only hear the parts that make them angrier.

In my experience, only a small part of the total communication between two people is about the meaning of the words we are speaking. The words provide a framework and structure for the ideas we are trying to get across. What people really focus on is the **tone of voice** and the **body language**.

The tone or sound in which people speak relays the emotional intensity behind the words. When someone speaks in an angry tone, the words change meanings completely. The question "what are you doing?" totally changes according to the tone in which it is said.

We can watch our tone and listen to ourselves when we speak to improve our communication skills. When I notice that my tone is starting to harden, I realize it might be a sign to take a timeout. As soon as my tone becomes louder than is acceptable in a restaurant, then I know that I have been triggered.

The tone with which we speak to our kids or partners can be condescending and will be heard that way no matter what we do to hide it. I have many clients who cringe when remembering their parent's tone of voice when talking to them. Just being aware of the damage that the wrong tone can inflict is sometimes enough to correct our actions before someone gets hurt.

When we are standing in front of someone, our body language says so much about our energy. If our arms are crossed, we show defiance and aggressiveness. If we lean forward to listen to someone, it shows that we are actively interested.

Paying attention to our words, tone and body language can hugely impact how we perceive and are perceived in the world. Think about how we are standing, our posture and the way our arms are placed. Think about our tone and the harshness in it. Take deep breaths and think about keeping our face smooth and open. The calmer we are, the more peaceful the situation will be as we are half of that situation.

Our good intentions can have a positive outcome if we are aware of all the forms of communication. The way we say things is just as important as what we are saying.

5. CONFLICT RESOLUTION

So far, we've learned that anger can be beneficial in relationships in that it can be a signal that a change is needed. We've also learned that most issues can be resolved by stating our position, then letting go. There are times, however, when conflict is inevitable. To properly deal with conflict, I've developed a six-step process to follow that will help you get through these issues in a peaceful way:

- **Step 1 – Identify the Conflict –** Correctly name what it is exactly you are in conflict about.

- **Step 2 – Confront the Source –** Pick the right time to deal with the issue in a rational way.

- **Step 3 – Be Precise –** Only talk about the exact thing you are in conflict about, nothing more.

- **Step 4 – Set Boundaries –** Make tangible guidelines and consequences.

- **Step 5 - Clarify and Negotiate -** Come to a mutual understanding about possible resolutions.

- **Step 6 - Let Go -** Forgive the conflict and move on in your lives.

The History

Bill, a 50-year-old software developer, came to me for counselling with issues of low self-esteem and depression. In one of our sessions, he opened up about his anger and the fights he got into with his wife, Judy. When they go to dinner parties, Bill likes to tell stories. When he is in the middle of the story, Judy constantly interrupts him to correct his facts. Judy feels justified because she "hates lies" and is ashamed because she thinks that Bill exaggerates and is inaccurate.

She tells herself that her reasons are noble because she doesn't want Bill to be thought of as a liar to their friends. What she doesn't realize is that her actions are doing the exact thing she is trying to avoid: shaming Bill.

Bill's anger toward Judy splashes over into brutal arguments and silence. Judy's anger, in turn, makes her resentful of Bill and causes her to respect him less. If this conflict is not resolved, they quickly step onto the escalator of anger.

Step 1 - Identify the Conflict

Before we get too far into the blame game, I want to reiterate that we all are responsible for our own anger. **No one makes us angry.** If we start pointing fingers before thinking about it and taking responsibility, then nothing will ever be resolved.

To correctly identify what the exact behaviour is that has upset your equilibrium, you have to stop and reflect. Put on the emotional brakes and think about what really is going on. When we are too fired up with emotion, none of us can see the situation with any clarity. If you can't focus on the situation, try writing it down in point form.

At this point, you have to determine if the issue is big enough to continue in the process. If you make a big deal about every little mistake, then eventually you won't be taken seriously. If the action is malicious against your mental, physical or emotional health, then you have to resolve it to avoid splashing.

When we sat down together, we realized that the problem was two-fold. Bill was exaggerating, and Judy was correcting him publically. Bill was not confronting her about the shaming that was happening between them and was taking out his anger on her in other ways.

Step 2 – Confront the Source (at the right time!)

Bill realized that there was a problem, but I had to ask him when the best time to confront Judy about it would be. Is it better to do it when you are feeling overly emotional, or is it better to wait until you are calm?

What are we taught to do in fire safety class if we catch on fire?

Stop…Drop…Roll. Let's use this as a model.

Stop fighting immediately when you feel emotional. **Drop** the subject for the moment. **Roll** with it and wait for a better time to be angry.

This can be the most difficult thing to do in a marriage or relationship. Trust me, I know. When our pails are full, all we want to do is release the pressure and spill out into a fight.

How has that worked for you so far? Has screaming at each other ever helped you resolve anything?

Be prudent when planning the confrontation. There is a time and a place for it, and that time and place is usually not when you are mad. Pick a later hour or the next day and plan to talk about the issue. Most of all make sure that you do it in private so that you will not be shaming each other and adding more to your pails.

Alcohol is sometimes a central issue and, if it is involved, wait until there is sobriety to start thinking about resolution. If the confrontation takes place when either party is drunk, then one or both sides are bound to get burned.

The next morning over coffee, Bill decides that it is worth the effort to try to change the pattern they have fallen into.

"Judy, I felt stupid the other night when you corrected me while I was telling a story. You basically called me a liar in front of all of our friends. I know that I can sometimes exaggerate, but you don't have to belittle me. It makes us both look like fools."

Step 3 – Be Precise – ONE ISSUE AT A TIME!!!

Bills expression of unhappiness is a trigger for Judy. She hates feeling like a fool and hates being called one. She quickly starts to talk about all the times that Bill has made her feel like a fool in public.

She wants to add fuel to the fire to get Bill on the escalator with her. By recounting all the sins of the past and making blanket statements, she attempts to justify her actions.

If you want to solve a conflict, then you have to deal with only that issue.

I cannot stress enough how important this is. As soon as you or your partner starts bringing in other past issues, then there can be no resolution.

I've found in my years of family counselling that the one who feels attacked for something they did or didn't do will almost immediately bring up something the other has done in the past to make it fair and to justify their actions.

This is why we can't be civil and honest with each other when trying to work things out. If we turn conflict resolution into a court of relationship, then both of you will always be thrown into jail for all the dirt you've wandered through.

People who have had their trust broken are especially susceptible to doing this. They start listing the ways the other person has broken their trust in the past as absolute proof of their guilt in the present.

In my course, I bring out a handful of pens and use them as an example. How can I write with the pen that is given to me in the moment if my hands are full with the pens of past moments? To write clearly, you have to hold only one pen at a time.

Use "I" statements as much as possible when being precise.

"Judy, I felt very uncomfortable the other night when you corrected me when I was telling my story. I might exaggerate when I talk, but that doesn't mean that I am a liar. I feel angry when you correct me and I want it to stop."

Communicating your precise feelings is a form of intelligence that we all must work on. Start practicing precision, and your fires will not blaze out of control.

Step 4 – Set Boundaries

At this point, Bill needs to set a boundary with Judy so that the pattern of correcting and shaming will be stopped.

What exactly is a boundary?

A boundary is a tangible barrier that can be measured, and when it is crossed, there are consequences. Boundaries empower both of you to be assertive about what you consider right or wrong behaviour in your relationship.

Boundaries must be specific to the issue. Don't let boundary setting become a way to control or be controlled by making massive boundaries. If you want something to work, then you have to start off small and specific.

It is essential for you to analyze the other person's perspective before a boundary is set. Most of the time, the problem exists because we do not understand where the other person or people in the conflict are coming from. This involves having an open mind to see things through their eyes and to take a walk in their shoes. It could be that your own stubbornness or unwillingness to compromise is the central issue.

Too many relationships fall apart because people want to play power games and be the dominant one in the pair. Be honest with yourself about what you see.

Lastly, make sure you include the consequence in the boundary so that the other person realizes what will happen if the boundary is crossed. It is only fair to give them warning about what will happen if the behaviour patterns continue.

Bill sets his boundary by saying, "I don't want to feel like a liar anymore. I want you to wait until we get home before you tell me what facts in my story were wrong."

"If you keep correcting me in public, then I'm going to stop telling the story right then or I will confront you like I'm doing right now about this matter in front of everyone. I don't want to shame you, but I don't want to be shamed either. I know you don't want us to look bad, but if you keep on correcting me, then I will correct your behaviour, too."

Step 5 – Clarify and Negotiate

Bill needs to stop and give Judy some time to think about what he is saying. She will have her own perspective, and his boundary setting might lead to another trigger.

If you sense that another trigger is about to take place, then calmly ask them to think about what you have said and stop the conversation. She might consider your boundary an ultimatum, and you will need to clarify.

The conflict is usually much more complicated that you think. For this reason, it is best to give yourself and the other person some time to come to a better understanding of what is really going on.

Judy needs to fully understand Bill's concerns and motivations if the process is going to work. If there is not understanding, then bitterness, resentment and retaliation will soon follow.

Judy is going to want to negotiate the boundary and what exactly it involves. She may think that the consequence is not in proportion to her correction, and that by correcting her, she is being shamed more than him.

Bill gives Judy an opportunity to negotiate the boundary and set her own.

Judy responds by saying, *"I hate it when you get the facts of the stories wrong. I don't want people to think you are lying to them when it doesn't make sense. I didn't realize that it was embarrassing you so much."*

Bill concedes, *"You know, sometimes I do get bit carried away with the details. I'll try to tone it down. If you think I'm going a bit over the top, then just give me a look and wait until we are in private before correcting me. If it is really important, then do it gently so that you protect me. We are on the same team, honey, and we have to look out for each other first."*

Step 6 – Let Go of Your Anger

To bring the peace back into the relationship, Bill and Judy both have to let go of their anger.

Once you have assertively changed the behaviour with firm instruction, you have to look in the mirror and accept the boundaries. Even if you perceive that you are in the right, the truth remains that you are not perfect and probably need to change, too.

In **Luke 6:27**, when Jesus told us that we should love our enemies as our friends and pray for them, I believe what he was saying was that we are not enemies. I've heard comedians joke about the fact that, as soon as you are married, it means you become enemies, working against each other for control.

This might be funny to think about, but it is sad to see how often it is true. In reality, you are on the same side, both striving for the same purposes and the same direction in life. You have to work together for real change instead of against each other.

We all need to accept the reality that **people are what they are**. We all fail in some parts of our life and nobody is perfect. If you really want your relationships to work, then you are both going to have to work together through these six steps. No one can resolve a conflict alone and remain together. There has to be unity for success to manifest itself in your life.

When the process is completed, try to end it with something positive, like a compliment or a similar personal touch, maybe a hug or handshake. This bonding moment solidifies the fact that anger can be worked through and solved. **There is always a hope of resolution.**

James 4:1-2 – "What causes fights and quarrels among you? Don't they come from those desires that battle within you? You want something but don't get it. You hate and covet, but you cannot have what you want. You quarrel and fight. You do not have because you do not ask God."

Exercise – Letting Go

Have you ever heard anyone to tell you to let it go? It probably bugs you when somebody says that; I know it used to bug me all the time. "You let it go!" I would want to scream back at them. I didn't want to let anything go, I wanted them all to realize what absolute idiots they were being (or that I was being when I did something wrong).

Many of these instances are the result of perceived injustices, misunderstandings or petty arguments that have no importance in the long run. Trying to prove who is right and who is wrong traps you into negative and escalating emotional situations that can easily be avoided. Focusing on injustice takes so much time and energy. Entitlement leads to the need to be in control or, worse yet, to win at all costs. Instead of letting things go, they feel like there was some injustice to be corrected or entitlement that leads to them light their fire of anger on the most trivial issues.

When you first start to let things go, it will be very hard, especially if you are as stubborn as I am. The key thing to remember is that it gets easier as you go. You don't even need to make a big deal about forgiving the little things in the world and go straight to forgetting them.

Assignment:

For the next two days, I want you to actively let things go. When someone does something that usually bugs you, just turn around, take a deep breath and forget that it ever happened. This is an experiment to start to show you that you don't have to always lose your temper over small things. Once you start, you might find that you don't want to let go of letting go.

PRAYER FOR RESOLVING CONFLICTS

LORD JESUS,

Forgive me for the multiple times I have charged ahead with my own agenda, regardless of the consequences of my anger. I pray that You will soften my heart, allowing me to step back and be rational in those times that I feel the anger building up inside of me. I desire to be a rational person, not a person who flies off the handle and hurts myself and others. I pray now that You would implant in my mind those six steps of conflict resolution that I have learned in this last chapter. Help me to remember to identify the conflict and not to be fragmented in my thoughts by bringing up other issues. Then, Lord, guide me in the right time and place to confront – allow me to step back and not wade into something that will be destructive to me and my loved ones. Keep my mind clear of all the other issues that might crop up and be able to stick to the issue at hand. Show me, Lord, where I need to set boundaries and what they need to be. Give me the patience I need to negotiate if need be and not to dig my heels in and be stubborn. And most of all, Lord, help me to let go of the anger. I am so accustomed to the feelings of anger that somehow it feels safer to keep on being angry rather than letting go and forgiving. Give me the strength I need to move on from this episode and bring the peace You promise.

AMEN.

6. WHEN ANGER BECOMES ABUSE

"Over my dead body will you ever do any counselling in this school!" *The principal yells out at me as I leave his office.*

I had just returned from a short sabbatical and received my degree in counselling. It was something that I was good at, and I knew it. Kids in my classes had started to ask me for advice about their lives, and I found that I loved helping them get through their issues. Nobody had been there for me, and I knew that I could use all I had learned to help out someone like me.

Yet every time I turned around, the principal of the school was putting me down, blocking my progress and treating me with condescension. The more praise I received from the parents and the community, the more he would give me a hard time.

It seemed as though things in all parts of my life were coming to a boiling point lately. Ever since that little German lady had come to the door preaching about Jesus, nothing had been the same. I was still partying on the weekends, but the liquor just didn't do it for me anymore. The next morning, it all felt so empty and stupid. MaryBelle was still fighting with me about my bad habits, and I thought that maybe if we made a move, it might help.

The principal is following me down the hall, letting me know that he's given the school counselling hours to someone else not nearly as trained as I am.

It was always hard for me to believe in myself – people had always been bringing me down. Finally I had found something that I was good at. I could listen to people's problems and figure out real solutions. No other job had felt so good or so right.

The principal had already given me a letter of reprimand focusing on a quote I had given in a letter to the graduating class. I had ended the message with a simple "God Bless You."

I knew right then that he was never going to let up.

I turned on my heel to face this man who was always on my case about something.

"You are right; I'm not going to be a counsellor in this school. I just got a job offer doing full-time counselling in another county. I was going to wait to give you my resignation, but I've had enough. I quit."

As I walk of the school, I feel something new growing inside of me. I don't need to suffer at the hands of other people who tell me I'm not good enough, who insult me for my beliefs and for my character.

I am finally doing it; I am breaking the cycle of abuse. I begin to realize that my prayers are being answered.

OUTWARD EXPRESSIONS OF NEGATIVE ANGER

When a full pail splashes onto the fires of anger, then there is a negative reaction that carries the intent of causing fear, pain or injury to ourselves or to others. Many times, this type of aggressive expression of anger is used to control others. The most recognizable expression is that of **violence**. Contrary to what many people think, violent expressions can not only be physical, but also verbal, sexual, religious and psychological. When a drunk man slaps around his wife, it is easy to recognize violence. When a bitter wife yells at her husband or a depressed mother belittles and shames her children, it is harder for us to recognize those aggressive expressions as violence.

As soon as I feel someone enter my personal space in order to dominate or control me, I immediately realize that the situation has become violent and that I need to set a boundary.

When the coach screams relentlessly at his team, it is a form of violence. When a bully torments his victim with cruel names or threats of harm, it is violence. When a pastor directs his sermon at a single person with condemnation, it is spiritual manipulation, which is a form of violence. When someone yells to cause fear, to intimidate or to control, it is a verbal form of violence. There are times when we must use a loud voice to set a boundary or protect our space, but as soon as we do it in an aggressive way, then it becomes a negative expression of our anger.

As soon as any situation becomes violent, a timeout should be called until the emotions of both sides are in order. There are times when someone may use violent actions that don't appear to be violent because they are calm when they do them. A father who pinches his children, flicks them in the head or utters condescending remarks to belittle them is displaying aggressive anger. They might even say things like "this is for your own good" when they commit this subtle form of violence.

Any form of sexual abuse is crossing a personal boundary to satisfy the abuser's needs. The abuser makes the victim an object in order to dehumanize them.

One of my clients used to play hockey and, while he was sitting on the bench, the coach would stand behind him and rub his penis against his back. That was an act of sexual violence toward the kid that made him question himself and eventually led to a divorce and insecurity about his sexuality. It may not seem like a violent act, but it affected him for the rest of his life. We often misconstrue sexual abuse as extreme when, in fact, it can be very subtle.

In all the forms of aggressive action, we must first and foremost recognize them for what they really are so that we can speak to them and bring about change.

The other most common face of negative anger is called **passive aggressive abuse.**

Passive aggressive behaviour occurs when a person feels angry towards someone but cannot express it in an aggressive or assertive way. It is like creating a wall of fire around ourselves so that we block out and stay behind that anger to gain control over the situation. Nobody penetrates our wall, and if they try, they get burned.

If someone tries to approach passive aggressive people, they will ignore, obstruct, procrastinate, become helpless or victimize themselves to get what they want. More than anything, if someone tries to touch them directly, then they burn you in one form or another.

The most common type of passive aggressive expression, and possibly the most hurtful, is the use of silence as a weapon. This silence creates ambiguity as to what we can or cannot change to help resolve the situation. Both parties are left powerless when silence is used as passive aggressive abuse.

I once counselled a young couple in which the woman would stop talking to her boyfriend if she even suspected that he was flirting with another woman. Days would pass, and the boyfriend wouldn't even know what he had done wrong.

Other forms of passive aggressive negative expressions of anger include: gossip, manipulation and deviance. These often subtle forms of behaviour can be devastating to relationships. Children watch passive aggressive behaviour and, later in life, act it out as if it is a normal way of expressing anger.

The Bible says it best in **Galatians 6:7**: "A man reaps what he sows." If you sow the seeds of negative anger into your life, then you will get negative consequences. When you are on the receiving end, it can trigger the flight-or-fight reaction.

INWARD EXPRESSIONS OF NEGATIVE ANGER

The first inward expression of repressed anger takes place entirely within the emotional realm of the individual. This is self-abuse and, when diagnosed, professional help is almost always needed. Breaking the cycle of internal abuse can be much more difficult than breaking that of external abuse.

Below are several examples of how negative emotions stored in our pails can splash inwardly to create mental illness.

Anxiety disorders are often the result of these internal splashes. The unreleased emotion can become a source of obsessive thinking and panic disorders because the individual does not know how to deal with all of those unresolved issues.

Depression occurs when the pail is so full that it appears like it will never be empty. Nothing can change the past, help in the present or prevent the future. This is the hopelessness caused by stored negative emotion that has nowhere to go.

Phobias are often the result of a past psychological injury that has built up over time and is triggered when outside circumstances are redirected inwardly. Anger reduction has been proven to lessen the magnitude of irrational fear in some instances.

Obsessive compulsive disorders may be initially formed out of a preoccupation with rules, lists and details. These compulsive patterns are used to control outward flares of anger, yet those same patterns can splash inwards until they control us.

Eating disorders, like anorexia and bulimia, can stem from anger at not being able to control our lives. That anger expresses itself through the control over one single issue: food. They feel that no one can control what they do or do not eat. They splash out their insecurities onto their own bodies, making themselves suffer for their powerlessness in other areas.

When anger is directed inward, the fire becomes psychosomatic and affects our physical well being. Some respiratory disorders, like asthma, can be set off by sudden rage attacks.

More obvious effects of anger are migraines, back aches and high blood pressure. Any time that distress enters your life, it can become apparent in signs like ulcers, eczema or insomnia.

Inward splashing of our full pails can be much more damaging to our physical and mental well-being than we could ever imagine. Anger affects all parts of our lives.

Psalm 107:17-18 – "Some became fools through their rebellious ways and suffered affliction because of their iniquities. They loathed all food and drew near the gates of death. Then they cried to the Lord in their trouble and he saved them from their distress. He sent forth his Word (Jesus) and healed them. He rescued them from the grave."

I gave this verse to a missionary kid who was hospitalized for anorexia. She asked me if God understood her condition. He gave me the above verse and through it we managed to work through her anger issues and allow healing to take place.

PRAYER FOR OVERCOMING NEGATIVE ANGER

LORD JESUS,
I have developed an obsessive pattern of feeling overwhelmed by life and resorting to negative patterns to get attention. Instead of looking at my problems individually and with reason, I panic and run to my husband and my friends to rescue me from these feelings

of helplessness. After doing this, I feel empty and ashamed and more alone than ever. I know I have become one of those people who 'use up' the compassion of others until they can't handle my needs any more.

Lord, help me to walk with You into my legitimate pain, to face what is hurting me, what is causing the anxiety, and to release it into You. Your yoke is easy, and You can easily carry my burdens. Help me to see that and believe it. This feeling of being overwhelmed is an addiction that I run to. I confess this and ask You, Lord, to remove the stronghold that keeps me from peace. Take away the idea that the problem is just too huge for me to handle. Help me to gain perspective. Give me the courage to seek guidance from those who can truly help me change my life.

AMEN.

THE ABUSE CYCLE IN RELATIONSHIPS

I had just sent Lisa to a safe house because her common-law husband had kicked her out and locked her out of her house in the middle of winter. This wasn't the first time this had happened. Since the beginning of her abusive relationship with Brian, she had been leaving him then going back.

Lisa had grown up in a home where her parents would fight, sometimes yelling, other times silence and, at the worst moments, there was violence. Lisa's low self-esteem, combined with this generational pattern, made it easy for her to slip into the abuse cycle.

An argument turns into yelling and then into screaming. A coffee mug is thrown, and a slap thunders across the kitchen. The police are called as the children sit in the flashing lights wondering if their parents will leave forever.

Approximately 1 in 8 Canadian women living with a male partner experience some kind of abuse from their partner.[1] Across Alberta, more than 12,000 women and children stayed in Alberta's shelters last year.[2]

Abuse can take many forms. It not only refers to physical violence but can be seen in sexual, emotional, verbal and psychological manipulation.

- **Phase One** is the increased tension that builds up in one or both partner's pails.

- **Phase Two** occurs when the splash and ignition take place. There is some form of violent abuse.

- **Phase Three** happens when the fire subsides and the abusive partner feels deep shame and asks to be forgiven. The abused partner is approached with promises of change.

- **Phase Four** is the honeymoon phase, filled with affection and excitement that things have really changed. This phase can be excellent with good parenting as they both try harder than ever to listen and care for each other. There is hope.

- **Phase Five** occurs when the insults and need for submissiveness start again. The threats begin, and both partner's pails start to fill up dangerously. Another splash is eminent. They move out of

1 Statistics Canada - www.statcan.gc.ca/pub/85-224-x/85-224-x2005000-eng.pdf

2 Government of Alberta – Children and Youth Services - www.child.alberta.ca/home/828.cfm

equilibrium and get too close to the fire. It is only a matter of time before everyone involved gets burned.

In my experience, abuse goes in a cycle and the steps can be documented. One of the ways of breaking this cycle is to look at it and realize what those steps are.

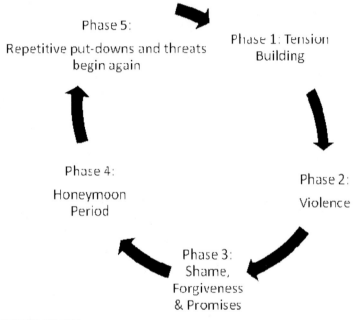

Phase 5:
Repetitive put-downs and threats begin again

Phase 1: Tension Building

Phase 4:
Honeymoon Period

Phase 2:
Violence

Phase 3:
Shame, Forgiveness & Promises

ABUSE CYCLE

The motor that spins this cycle is fuelled by **fear** (of being alone) and **denial** (that it is as bad as it really is). The abused is usually unaware of their options, and the people in their lives don't ask the questions that would help them break the silence of abuse. Our culture and society is just now starting to put value on helping these women. Often governments don't give enough resources, and society turns a blind eye in shame.

This cycle can be and is mapped according to frequency and intensity. In some families, it takes three to six months to run a rotation, but in others, it can happen in days.

WHY DO PEOPLE STAY TOGETHER IN THIS ABUSIVE CYCLE?

We Teach People How to Treat Us

Because they have been taught by their parents to take the minimum out of relationships, they cling to a false hope that things will get better. Lisa was never taught to identify abnormal behaviours and set boundaries. She was taught to take responsibility for the feelings of the abusive partner. Lisa feels that she needs to justify and explain her actions to Brian, just as her mother did with her father. Finally, they feel an incredible amount of shame that somehow they are really the ones at fault for the defective relationship.

We teach people how to treat us. When people come from dysfunctional homes, they may have certain characteristics that teach people to treat them in a negative way.

Not Recognizing Abnormal Behaviours

For a start, we don't always recognize abnormal behaviours and set boundaries for them. When a friend loses his temper and screams at us, we don't stop and think, "Hmmm, that wasn't cool, I'm not going to take that kind of thing in my life." Instead, we think back to our father who used to scream at everyone whenever anything went wrong. We think in our head, "People are just like that. He's got his good points, too. Everybody loses it sometimes."

It may be partially true that everyone loses their temper, but it is important to recognize when people are abusive and mean with their anger. It is important to be able to identify when people are manipulating or lying to you to protect themselves or to gain an advantage over you.

Recognizing that something isn't right automatically teaches people that if they want your respect, they better treat you with the same respect. If they don't give you respect, then you need to decrease the effect of their relationship to you. People within our family are hard to set boundaries with as they think they can do whatever they want. To get respect from them, it is imperative that we still set boundaries.

Taking Responsibility

Another characteristic of abuse is taking responsibility for the abuser's emotions. This allows other people to blame us for their emotions and to do disrespectful and hurtful things and then cast that responsibility on us. When we make people accountable for their emotions and actions, they will be less likely to be so careless.

I've learned that some of the anger in my pail was due to the fact that I was not living up to the lie that I needed to make my wife happy. She had a tendency to put me in charge of her happiness, and Christianity became another tool that told me that I needed to be in charge of her happiness. Even in the darkest times with my parents, I believed that I could take charge and make them happy. I tried to take charge to avoid conflict and learned to take responsibility.

If the brain is like a computer, then we each have a certain number of emotional responses that open when we click on the right icon. We hold the mouse that chooses a direction in which happiness is the end result. I cannot be responsible for your computer and the choices you make with your mouse.

When I think about it like that, I realize that no matter what I do in my life, I cannot control my wife's happiness, sadness, goodness or joy. She is responsible for choosing the actions in her life that produce the emotions she wants to have.

Accepting the Minimum

When coming from a dysfunctional upbringing, we have a tendency to accept the minimum in relationships. We give out love and only expect the bare minimum in return. If you could measure love in units, it's like we give out 50 units and are happy when only one or two is returned. We tolerate abuse and disrespect if at least some acceptance is given back.

Sadly, many people fall into relationships with severely angry partners and get trapped in them. Those partners wear away at our self-esteem until we start to feel that we are pretty lucky to be loved by one person in the world. They know how flawed we are and still love us, so it's easy to accept the fact that they get drunk every night. They affirm that nobody will ever love us, and because we are used to taking the minimum, we believe this lie.

If you normally make $20 an hour for your work, would you suddenly accept $1 an hour for the same work? When we emotionally invest in others, we should be rewarded in kind.

Look around you, open your eyes. There are thousands of people in the world that won't treat you so badly and give you the bare minimum in return for your love. To break free of that thinking, you have to first be whole and healthy in yourself, and you have to work on not needing another person to lean on to be happy. Once you can stand on your own, you will start giving and taking the love you deserve.

Justifications and Explanations

Why do we need to justify and explain all of our actions? Is there some kind of guilt that has been painted on your soul so that you feel like you need to show that everything you do has a reason and is not wrong just because you do it? The need to be understood allows others to use your own words against you and to suspect your motivations. Every action does not need to be justified. Go through your life and cast off the negative feelings that you project on the world, and soon you will find that your steps lead to brighter times.

An abusive person will listen to 100 points of justification to find the one point that is questionable. That one point will become their focus of attack. We have to remind ourselves that no means NO and that we don't need to explain it to abusive people.

Internalization of Blame

The last characteristic that I will mention (although there are plenty more) is the internalization of blame. Children of dysfunctional homes have feelings of guilt and shame whenever there is a conflict. When people are fighting, we automatically think that we are somehow to blame. When something goes wrong, we immediately think it's our failing.

Unless the above five characteristics are challenged and changed, we will retain the neon sign on our foreheads that attracts abusive people to us. We might leave one abusive relationship only to fall right into the next. I have had clients that have had up to five or six abusive relationships before they tore down the neon sign that says, "Abuse me."

It's true that some things really are our fault, and I encourage taking responsibility for them, but saying "sorry" just because something goes wrong only leads you into the rabbit hole of blame.

Manipulating the Angry Spouse

I have found on some occasions that there is a counter manipulation that occurs when someone splashes out with fire. After the explosion, all their fuel is gone, burned away. Their personal power is drained and their self-esteem runs low while shame runs high.

At this stage, the abused partner has a tremendous amount of rage at being a victim to someone they have a relationship with. They see that the abuser is weak and use that moment to take advantage of them by making them agree to doing or buying something they wouldn't normally do or buy. They subtly attack their self-esteem in order to gain more control in the relationship.

The sad thing is that those manipulations only turn into more fuel for the fire and can even be another trigger to start the cycle again. So many couples are stuck in the cycle of anger, and it is one of the hardest to break because of the excitement and intensity of emotion.

Most of our issues don't come to abuse. They are conflicts that can be dealt with in a reasonable way. I have come up with some steps to help you resolve these issues before they escalate into abuse.

> *1 Peter 3:8-9* – "Live in harmony with one another; be sympathetic, love as brothers, be compassionate and humble. Do not repay evil with evil or insult with insult, but with blessing, because to this you were called so that you may inherit a blessing."

HEALING PRAYERS FOR BREAKING THE CYCLE OF ABUSE

Abused person's prayer:

LORD JESUS,
I cry out to You to bring this cycle of abuse in our relationship to an end. You have been witness each time it starts and through each stage as the anger inflames and spreads. Help me to see it plainly as a cycle, as something that takes on a life of its own and will repeat itself if I don't change the way I react. Give me the

strength to remember the stages so that I can get off the escalator of anger before it goes to the next more violent stage. Give me courage when I feel weak, strength to stand up and be heard, yet making sure I am in a safe place. Please put someone that I can trust in my path so I have somewhere safe to go and someone I can feel I can talk to. I am trusting You, Lord, to end this cycle for me.
AMEN.

Abuser's prayer:

LORD JESUS,
I do not know how I got to be in this place I am now, a person who hurts those who have been entrusted to my care. I know that I want to change and be the person You created me to be. I am so tired of my anger and the cycle of abuse that I inflict. I pray that You will instill in me those gifts of Your Spirit that can change me into someone I can be proud of and not live in the shame I feel after I explode with anger. I know, Lord, that it will take a lot of work to change, but I am willing.
AMEN.

7. Counteracting the Causes and Effects of Negative Anger

Developing Good Self-Esteem

Anger can be devastating, and there are many ways to deal with it after the fact, but there are also ways to prevent it from happening. Many of our anger issues or our allowance of other's anger stems from low self-esteem.

Like any quality, self-esteem can be built up and nurtured. I have developed some strategies that you might want to try if you feel that you have low self-esteem.

Take Risks

My childhood was one of poverty and uncertainty, so taking risks is one of the hardest things I've ever had to do in my life. Once I started taking risks, I realized that the more risks I took, the more abundant and rich my life became.

As human beings, we tend to hold what we have close to our chests, not risking the little security we have accumulated. What most people don't understand is that the feeling of security grows the more risks you take. Excitement is so essential to living a full life that if you always play the safe card, then you will inevitably start to feel bad about yourself.

Exercise – Reach Out and Contact Someone

Call an old friend that you haven't talked to in a long time. Take the risk of reconnecting with someone you are afraid to talk to because of the distance. Even if the results are not what you wanted, the effort itself will build the strength of abundance inside you.

Receive

It took me years to be able to accept affirmations with a simple "thank you" instead of immediately deflecting them into self-criticism. It can be so hard on our pride to receive love and encouragement from others, especially when we don't think we deserve it.

The more you receive, the more you can give. The more you give, the easier it becomes to receive. When our self-esteem is low, it is so hard to receive compliments or advice. Our bad feelings about ourselves become a wall that nothing can penetrate to build the light on the inside.

Take what people want to give you freely and freely shall you both give and grow. If you do not accept what people have to give, then you are denying them the blessing of giving.

Exercise – Receiving

For the next five days, take whatever people offer you with a smile and a genuine thank you. At the same time, start giving yourself compliments, presents and encouragement and actively receive those things without guilt, looking in your mirror, smiling at your own face and saying thank you.

Protecting Yourself

John 10:3 states "The watchman opens the gate for him and the sheep listen to his voice. He calls his own sheep by name and leads them out." It means that we are to listen to the voice of the Good Shepherd and not focus on the negative voices.

It's so easy to just slink away when some jerk comes along and tries to take you down. There are those who suck out your goodness like psychic vampires. They need to drain your positivity to feed their own spiritual holes.

People cannot walk all over you if you are standing up. You have to look them in the eye and deny their negativity in an assertive way. Start small and work towards an assertive dedication where you don't let anyone belittle you or make you feel bad about yourself.

The next time you feel that someone is trying to suck your positive energy, stand up and walk away without giving them an explanation. If they protest about your sudden departure, just thank them for their time and leave any way.

In certain circumstances, you could give them a hug and a smile on your way out. Love the hell out of them. It is what Jesus would want you to do. You can love and protect yourself at the same time.

Do Your Best and Embrace the Results

Life is short, and with each and every moment, God gives us the opportunity to do the best we can with what we have. When we try our hardest to do the good we ought to do, there is a feeling of connection with the sacred in the moment of doing.

We can accept our limitations but push them so that, in the end, we feel that no matter what the outcome is, we have given it our all. Failure in life is unavoidable, and there is nothing we can do to prevent loss. Yet, if we do our best and live our lives to the fullest, the failure does not taste as bitter and the losses can instead be looked at as an avenue to wisdom.

Embrace yourself and embrace the results of your actions when you fully commit to being the best person you can be in that moment. This sort of mentality makes you beautiful in your own world.

PRAYER FOR COUNTERACTING NEGATIVE ANGER

LORD JESUS,
I know that it says in **Psalm 139** that I am fearfully and wonderfully made, but most of the time I don't believe that at all. For much of my life, I have felt like You made a mistake with me, I am so full of imperfections. My immediate response to negative

remarks and implications is to embrace them and believe that they are true, which leads me to hating myself more. Help me, Lord, to first of all embrace the truth that I was created by You and that I am not a mistake. Help me to not take those negative remarks and insults as truth but to put in perspective that they are only another's opinion. I can discard others' opinions and not embrace them as the truth.

Help me to build myself up daily by affirming myself as a child of God, a person worthy of love and acceptance. Allow me to quickly recognize negativity as it is put in front of me and be given the strength to walk away. Please, Lord, embed in my mind those five common characteristics of people who are in a cycle of abuse and help me to recognize them in those situations that happen in my relationships. I want to be able to come into my relationships in a healthy, functional way and to discard the dysfunction that now controls me and my family. I pray for someone to come into my life that can walk with me as I embrace the healing you have for me.

AMEN.

Psalm 139:13-14 – "For you created my inmost being, you knit me together in my mother's womb. I praise you because I am fearfully and wonderfully made."

Exercise – Give Yourself Some Credit

Start small and work up from there. The next time you have to do something, concentrate on ignoring your self-doubt and commit yourself completely to every action. Even if it doesn't come out exactly how you like, pat yourself on the back for the amazing effort you put into it. If you fail miserably at the task, then give yourself a pat on the back anyways for trying. Build into your mind a pattern of congratulating yourself in everything you do, as long as you have tried your hardest at it. Soon, you will be more likely to try things you've never tried before and might even feel good about them. Give it a shot!

8. Patterns That Trap Us

"Why are you so hard on me? I get straight A's, and I'm not going to do anything bad at the game. Why don't you ever trust me?"

It was the summer of 1993, and my son John was just going into Grade 12. He wanted to go out with his friends to a national soccer match at the stadium in Quito, Ecuador. I knew that John and his friends would be drinking. We were in our third year on the mission field, and every year he got more and more rebellious.

"I don't trust you because I know you are going out and partying. You are going to stay at Alain's house and his parents let you drink and smoke. This place is like a goldfish bowl. Everybody sees what you do, and I don't need that kind of judgement on me and my work."

"This isn't about you and your work, Dad. Everything is not about you and your work."

"If a man can't control his own house, then how can he be a witness for the Lord?"

"Why do you have to make everything about the Lord? This is about a stupid soccer game. I can't believe you are doing this. You make me so mad."

"I do this for your own good, John. You don't know how good you have it. My father used to beat me to a pulp."

I could feel the tears well up inside me thinking back to when I was his age. My father died the year I graduated from high school. He had tried to send me letters, but I sent them all back unopened, cursing him in bold letters on the back. The day I heard he died, I wanted to jump off the bridge near my house. I had nothing, my mother had kicked me out, and I didn't even have an extra pair of jeans.

"You are so ungrateful. If you only knew how hard I had it then..."

"I know how hard you had it because you remind me every minute you disagree with me. So what if your dad beat you. You are beating me up emotionally with your control of me."

The words resounded in my head, and like a fireball exploding, my hands gripped his shoulders and started shaking.

"Go on and beat me, Dad. You are just like Jack, so be that way."

I let go and fall back against the wall. The door slams and I hear my wife come downstairs.

"What is going on here? Are you picking on John again? Why can't you ever leave him alone, he's just a kid?"

I want to yell and scream and fight like mad, but instead the silence takes me again and I go into the bathroom, locking the door and locking them all out.

My life had changed so drastically in the past five years that it was hard to even recognize the person I had been. After committing our lives to Christ, our family was taken on a high-speed roller coaster ride that swung us from language school in Texas to our mission posting in Ecuador. For the first year, I was counselling native Ecuadorians in the small city of Cuenca, while my two oldest kids, Brandy and John, were put into dorms in a missionary school for children in Quito.

The transitions were hard on all of us. Being separated for the first time caused incredible pain and insecurity on both sides. We were expected to be perfect Christians, and yet the same patterns that had plagued me before in my life were still there, making negative impacts in my life.

By the second year, the Lord gave us an opportunity to move to Quito, where I would counsel out of the missionary kid school where my eldest were attending. I quickly found that the most dedicated of Christian families were no different than us and struggled with the same devastating pails of stored emotions and the same patterns that had been passed on from generation to generation.

NEGATIVE PATTERNS THAT ARE LEARNED AND REPEATED

There are negative patterns that we have taken from our upbringing and are passing on to our children. These are learned by us when we are unable to see the truth, and if not dealt with now, they will be passed on to our children and to our grandchildren.

The Cycles of Generational Sin

One of the most common and tragic patterns is that the people who have been abused become the exact same monsters as the ones that hurt them. It is like zombies or vampires biting their victims and passing on the same horrible affliction.

Move on – Dead Ends and New Beginnings

Most people want to work things out and, especially where marriage is concerned, we are encouraged to do our most to make our covenant stick. There are times, though, when one person is not willing or cannot come to a resolution regarding the issues that keep you both unhappy.

With marriage, I always recommend separation before throwing it all away. The separation is to bring the resistant party to the full realization of what he or she is going to lose. It also makes both sides see what it is like to be without the stress of anger.

This could also be the case with friends or partners at work. When you can see that no resolution is possible, then you need to accept that it is over. We cannot spend our lives being miserable and must move on.

When some people are offended by us, they will never let go of the injustice they feel. We alone allow people to steal our joy. When someone won't forgive you or forget the past, it is useless to keep trying to convince them to do so, and you must move on.

Read *Matthew 7: 6* – "Do not give dogs what is sacred; do not throw your pearls to pigs. Don't waste your pearls on the pigs." Many times, we are trying to push our ideas or love on people that do not want or deserve them. Realize that not everyone will like you and move on.

Angry people can be abused by others' behaviours but can also be abusive in their own behaviours. The cycle of abuse is common in all forms.

I swore that I would never become abusive like my dad. Instead of breaking the patterns, however, I used and abused alcohol, put other people's needs ahead of mine and used negative anger on the ones closest to me. The nightmare became real when I woke up one day and realized that I was my dad. At 32 years old, my wife was threatening to leave me, and it hit me that alcohol and anger had taken control of my life.

I gave up alcohol for 10 years as a choice to break that pattern. You, too, can choose to change your life to break the cycle of abuse. Jesus gave me the strength and freedom to break free of this negative cycle of abuse.

TRIANGULATION

"Triangulation" is the word I use when there is an unresolved conflict between two people and a third person is involved. The third person almost always becomes the recipient of the anger that exists between the other two people. Instead of dealing with it directly, the warring couple brings in a third person to avoid direct conflict and any chance of resolution. At first, it may seem like a very complicated pattern, but the reality is that almost every family uses triangulation at one point or other.

The most prominent example in my life is when I am triangulated with my wife concerning issues over my son. I've always had high expectations for him, and whenever I'd discipline him, his mother, my wife, would quickly come to his defence and attack me for being hard on him. When the problem was really between my son and me, triangulation made it about the three of us and nothing was resolved.

Here is a diagram to show how triangulation works:

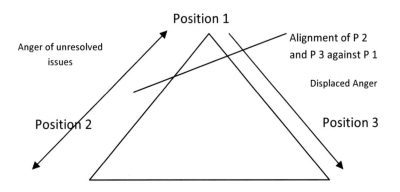

Position 1 – The person who has the anger issue. They may be the raging alcoholic or the defensive personality, have an eating disorder or other negative conditions that they do not want to deal with. The line represents that issue that is blocking them from a healthy life.

Position 2 – The co-dependent person who buys into the anger issue and enables it. They cannot confront it directly. The anger cycle continues, but the splash is directed at Position 3.

Position 3 – This person aligns with Position 2 against the one with the main anger issue (Position 1). As a result, this person is the main recipient of the splash from the conflict.

There may be a closer bond between 2 and 3, but it is in that bond where the resentment lies.

(As a side note, in these situations the anger issue concerns all three positions and all three need to look at their own anger, which may take many forms.)

Example – Against the Father to the Son

In this example, there is an unresolved issue of alcoholism that has existed throughout the marriage. The co-dependent wife, Beth (Position 2), grew up in a home with an alcoholic father, and then she married Charles (Position 1), who had his own addiction to the drink. She was used to accepting the bare minimum in relationships, not setting boundaries and taking full responsibility for raising her many children.

The first son, Ian (Position 3), had tremendous amounts of pressure put on him by his father, Charles. Ian was a shy individual who wasn't as physical as his father. He was expected to be outgoing, strong, successful and a stand-up guy in the community.

Ian couldn't live up to those expectations, so Charles picked on him mercilessly, putting him down with belligerent insults when he got drunk. Beth hated it when Charles drank and would defend her son but never confronted Charles about his drinking. Ian became the central issue in their marriage, and the more she defended him, the more Charles became determined to see his son as a failure.

Eventually, Ian broke down and followed the generational pattern of self-medication, becoming a severe alcoholic. The displaced anger of his parent's failed marriage was put on his shoulders, and it was too much to bear.

To this day, Charles has contempt for anything Ian does. He can hardly stand to be in Ian's presence. Beth still holds anger towards Charles and tries to protect Ian and take responsibility for him. They have triangulated Ian and crippled him because they could not face the real issues in their marriage.

If they had only addressed the real issue of Charles's drinking and the unrealistic expectations he put on Ian, they might have helped drain Ian's ever-filling pail as well as their own. Their marriage continued, but the love between them had long extinguished.

There are many other examples of triangulation that are apparent in our lives. A father may triangulate with his daughter against the mother who has intimacy issues or, in a larger family, a group of tightly knit sisters may triangulate against their brother-in-law out of jealousy.

Each triangulation issue has its own unique qualities, but the failure to directly resolve the conflict between the two parties with the issues always leads to collateral pain.

In each of these situations, God can speak into them and bring change. The majority of times, just seeing the reality of triangulation in their lives can bring about an effort to change it. The conflicting parties will finally confront their real issue. Afterwards, they should ask forgiveness from the triangulated party that has received the brunt of negative anger.

More often than not, I have to teach Position 3 to remove themselves completely from Position 1 and 2. They feel relieved that they no longer have to be in such a key role and can release the anger that they have stored because of it.

Triangulation is a common problem in many families, and it is one that can scar all three sides if not recognized and resolved. Children that are triangulated with divorcing parents are often forced to choose a side but still go between the parents. This kind of triangulation is sure to add unhealthy emotions to any child's pail. For this reason, we must do our best to express our anger to the person that is involved in it and not foist it upon innocent bystanders.

PRAYER FOR TRIANGULATION

LORD JESUS,

As I read through this section on triangulation, I recognized that this is a trap that my family and I have fallen into. I recognize that my _____ and I often get together and gang up on my _____. We have formed an unhealthy bond that is destroying our relationships. Give me the strength, Lord, to recognize when I am stepping into this pattern and the ability to step back from it, even though like ruts in a road, it would be so easy to go back in and continue with these destructive patterns.

Help me and _____
to stand together as husband and wife and be obedient to the good we need to do in the situation. Help us to look at our own marriage and see what needs to change and give us the desire to change things. Lord, help me to recognize triangulation in all its forms in our family

and to remember what I have learned, and then to gently instruct my family members in the way that we should go.

AMEN.

RANDOM REINFORCEMENT

"Random Reinforcement" describes the chaotic responses that lead to insecurity when parents give their children both love and expressions of negative anger at random intervals without reason. There is no justification as to why a reward is withheld or the punishment is given.

It's like having a candy machine that only gives candy some of the time. Abusive parents that only give love at random and inexplicable times build a level of insecurity that can affect their children for the rest of their lives.

We learn to take the minimum of what is deserved and are vulnerable to being abused. I grew up in an environment in which my mom would randomly reinforce me with praise when I did housework for her. She would also randomly ask me to leave the house for no reason. Other times, my mom would be super critical of my work even though it was exactly the same as before. I never knew what was going to happen with her.

I compare random reinforcement to Video Lottery Terminals. Gambling addicts and children become addicts to the uncertainty of the response.

This pattern gave me strong undercurrents of self-doubt as to whether I was doing a good enough job. Even at my current age, I still struggle with accepting the rewards of my labours.

I have repeated this pattern with my son. I don't know how to be consistent in rewarding him for his efforts. He'll work for me, and I won't pay him regularly but at random intervals. Even though he doesn't complain, I know that it bothers him.

As adults, we must realize that it is not normal for people to only give us love when they randomly feel like it. We need to look at the candy machine as being broken instead of turning it back on ourselves.

What I tell people is that we all have to quit going to machines that don't give us regular rewards and instead find the people that want to encourage and support us in what we do. When we recognize this pattern in ourselves with our own children, it is essential to consciously give both affirmation and punishment to them while explaining our reasons.

OBJECTIFICATION

"Objectification" is the process of turning people into ideas or objects so that it is easier to deal with our damaged emotions concerning them. It is easier to see someone as an object than to see them for the unique individuals that they are.

Violence and abuse are common when people become objects. Most criminals of sexual or violent nature turn their victims into objects. It is unlikely that a person will abuse a child sexually or physically when they see them as a little person with a name and a future. During angry outbursts, we make people into objects so we can ignore their human needs. My dad would objectify me with silence for weeks at a time. I had no power to stop his actions of making me non-existent. Seeing someone for who they really are makes it tougher to violate them.

Most objectification happens on the everyday level. When a man lusts after a pretty girl, he is seeing her body parts and not someone's daughter or sister. When a parent screams at their child, telling them that they are "nothing," they are seeing them as a "brat" and not their own flesh and blood.

A common form of objectification can be found in the roles we give people. It is easy to reject a father for being a bad father because he doesn't fit the role that we assign to him. He does not fit into all the expectations and limitations of that role.

When we can finally see our parents as individuals that have their own struggles and private demons, then suddenly it becomes much easier to accept them for who they are. In turn, parents often have plans for their kids to become doctors or lawyers and are angry when they want to be artists. If they open their eyes to the truth, they will see their children as the beautiful, unique individuals that they really are and a friendship can form.

This generational sin is a pattern that is passed on from father to son and mother to daughter. We must break this cycle by not turning the people we love into objects to justify our deeds. Making people into objects only limits them and our relationship with them.

SHAME AS A BELIEF SYSTEM

"Shame" is a negative way of viewing yourself when you do not measure up to standards that have been accepted as true. Sometimes, it stems from a traumatic event in your past, and other times it's passed on from your parents. It is like a blanket that is draped over your light because you do not feel like others will accept you.

Depression occurs when the feelings of being deficient, defective and unworthy preoccupy your whole being. Negative self-talk becomes incessant, repeating the lie that we weren't good enough in our past, we are not good enough today and we will never be good enough. We pass this on to our children, telling them without words that they aren't good enough either.

When I was in high school in Kitimat, BC, I brought one of my friends, Peter, home to my house. My dad got drunk and obnoxious. Halfway through the night, Peter phoned his mom to come and get him. Peter informed me later that week that his parents didn't want us to be friends anymore.

I was ashamed of my family and didn't invite another friend into my house. Even today, I find myself hiding aspects of my life away in fear that the community will reject me like Peter did. Even though I have hundreds of friends that accept me, I continue to struggle with wanting to fit in.

If not for the strong will of my children and our decision to love them unconditionally (as much as we can), I might have passed that shame on. Instead, our home became very open to their friends, and I learned to let go of that shame.

Jesus died to release us from shame, guilt and doubt, and if you can give that up to the cross, then you will be free. Jesus loves us for who we are, and it is our duty to fully love ourselves. If we love ourselves, we can rid ourselves of any generational shame. My own struggles with shame have given me the ability to counsel people and they feel no judgement from me. As Jesus loves me, so I love them.

The angry splashes that occur in our families can be the most devastating. Children look up to us and follow our leads in life. They trust us and expect us, as parents, to give them security. For us as adults, our parents are just as important in our lives, even if it is the absence of them. The family unit is where the fires of anger can destroy the kind of love that we all need in our lives: unconditional love.

A parent's love for their children is the closest thing we can see to God's love for us. It is the idea that we would give our lives for our children. Most of us, because of our stored anger and negative patterns, cannot see how to get to this love. Instead, we ignore the call of the Holy Spirit and justify our hurtful actions toward our children, our parents and our siblings.

Many times, it is the hurtful actions of those we are closest to that adds the most negative anger to our pails. It is these family members that we trust who have wounded, betrayed or used us to the point where we feel we cannot live normal lives.

Within families, there are systems that can be observed and changed. The irrational thinking and patterns that develop can be challenged and new ways of living with and loving each other can be formed.

9. NONCOMPLIANCE – NOT WANTING TO DO YOUR PART

Families have to work as a unit, and each member has to do their part. Both adults have to do a fair share of the work and take a fair share of the responsibilities. Children have to listen to their parents and do the tasks necessary to fulfill their part of the unit.

Anger comes when one or more family members flatly refuse to help out or do what they are asked. Immediately, there is a power struggle that invariably leads to a trigger, and then the whole family is caught on the escalator of anger.

Noncompliance occurs when one person is not responding to another person's request. There are two main ways this is expressed:

The person does not do the requested behaviour to a reasonable standard.

The person does not respond in a reasonable amount of time.

NONCOMPLIANCE IN CHILDREN

Some kids seem to want to challenge everything their parents ask them to do. Either the parents relent and transfer that anger to other relationships or screaming matches ensue. In some extreme examples, non-compliant children can destroy marriages. Their parents start triangulating the child's behaviour and unleash their frustrations on each other.

Most behavioural excesses and deficits in our children appear to revolve directly or indirectly around one type of core behaviour. This behaviour is what I define as **noncompliance**.

A noncompliant child shows defiant, hostile or negativistic behaviour. Four or more of the following might apply:

- Losing temper
- Arguing with adults
- Actively defying or refusing to carry out the rules or requests of adults
- Deliberately doing things that annoy others
- Blaming others for their own mistakes or misbehaviour
- Being touchy or easily annoyed with others
- Being angry and resentful
- Being spiteful or vindictive

If noncompliance can be reduced in children, then other inappropriate behaviours such as crying, throwing tantrums and aggressive behaviours will also stop. Positive parenting starts by reducing noncompliance in behaviourally disordered children before dealing with other behavioural deficits. If you catch your teenage son smoking, you have to think to yourself, "I need to teach my child how to follow my commands before I look at the smoking issue."

There is a relationship between noncompliance and the win-lose model. In both, there is no other option in the situation other than to win everything or lose everything.

All children use the win-lose model when they don't want to do something that they are asked to do. Behaviourally disordered children use it more frequently and with a greater intensity. In avoiding the task, they use tantrums, excuses, arguing and delays to win.

It is better to stop noncompliance in the early phases when the child is ignoring or delaying the instructions. Children do not always win the win-lose game. Behaviourally disordered children, though, may win a majority of the time.

If a constant system of dealing with the behaviour is not in place, then there is the **random reinforcement** that we talked about earlier. This pattern will lead to future negative anger for the children and you.

This is how a conversation with a noncompliant child usually goes:

Adult: *"Would you like to clean your room today, honey?"*

Child continues to play video games without responding in any way.

> Adult: *"Come on, baby, you know you have to clean your room today, sweetie."*

> Child: *"Just a minute, Mom, can't you see I'm busy? I'll do it later."*

> Adult: *"Don't use that tone of voice with me. You had better clean your room, or else."*

> Child: *"Or else what? You are going to cry? I'm busy playing my game, leave me alone. My room is clean enough already."*

> Adult: *"You are such a little brat. I can't believe that such a little demon ever came out of me. I'd like to just take you over my knee right now and…"*

This is where the splash happens. The child might wake up to the response, but it is too late. The escalator has already reached the crisis phase.

There are steps that you can follow to stop either side from being triggered. Remember to **keep your sails down** at all times so that you do not become emotionally involved in their noncompliance.

Step 1: Make Specific Demands

The first mistake that parents make when dealing with noncompliant children is to speak in a very general, non-specific way, usually in the form of a question. This ambiguous request gives the child a choice to ignore the request or just say no.

The mom articulated a poorly defined request: "Would you like to clean up your room today?"

The correct request would be: "It's time right now to clean up your clothes on the floor, make your bed and organize your desk. Please."

I've found that using a polite command is the best way to start off. I like to throw a "please" on the end to give proper respect to them, but I say it in a way so they know it is not a request. The responsibility is given with due respect and the expectation of completion.

At this point, if there is not an acknowledgement or movement towards the requested task, then the consequences should be given.

"If you don't start cleaning your room within the hour, I'm going to take away your video game console for the rest of the day."

Usually, this is where the child will try to win the argument by becoming super obnoxious. They'll start to scream and throw a tantrum. Parents often withdraw the request or are triggered onto the escalator. Either of these responses will create negative reinforcement.

If the parent remains specific and firm, then the child will understand the direction and the consequences.

Praise the child if there is compliance. Many parents have a belief that they should not praise the child or it will go to their heads. In reality, it makes the child acknowledge the worth of compliance. Tell them they are doing a good job or express your gratitude if they do what you tell them to do. If they do not, go to the next step.

Step 2: Give Them Time

After stating your specific demands, it's best to walk away to avoid any escalation of conflict. Many parents do not give their children enough time to process the request and the consequences of noncompliance. Usually, they stay in the situation and continue to nag and push. This creates an immediate escalation and gives the child more power to push back.

Remove yourself for a few minutes so that they have time to think. The more times a child is asked to do something, the less likely the child will follow through and comply.

Step 3: Request Using "Need"

When you return the second time and find them still in front of the television playing video games, it is time to intensify the request. Give them the same assertive command but use the phrase, "I *need* you to…" to add force to your words.

> Adult: "I *need* you to turn off your video games and start cleaning up your clothes, making your bed and organizing your desk. If you don't go now, then I'm taking the video game away."

Give them another 30 seconds, and if they respond into action, then go ahead and still give verbal reinforcement. If they still do not reply, then it is time to deliver the consequences.

Step 4: Deliver the Consequence

This is the hard part and where many parents give in. The consequence must be acted on or the pattern of random reinforcement continues.

I've found the best punishment is to take away some privilege that they take for granted. Taking away the connection cord for their video games or shutting off power to their room can be very effective. Kids today have a reliance on electricity and taking away those things is a very effective way of getting their attention.

This is where they are going to lose control of their temper in order to bully you into giving up the consequence. Little kids will start to cry and scream at the top of their lungs. Older kids will lash out with vicious insults or give you the silent treatment and run out of the house.

Don't give in! This is the moment where you have to show backbone. If you give in, you are teaching them that they can push you around and have more power than you do in the relationship. They make the situation win-lose, but if you want to break their negative patterns, you have to win.

Give them five minutes to cool down, and then redo steps 1 through 3. This time, they know you are serious so they might comply.

If they do comply, don't yell at them or make them feel bad. Even if it is hard, encourage them for complying with your request. Positive reinforcement is the best tool for future compliance.

Step 5: Continue to be Firm

So you've taken away the video game, but your child still isn't cleaning their room. An hour or two later, they come to you begging for the connection cord back. Many parents that I've counselled break down at this point. They are afraid their children won't love them and want to please them by giving in.

If weakness is shown, then the noncompliant child will have the upper hand in future conflicts. You have to hold out with the consequence to give it sufficient time to sink in. They have to know that you aren't joking around. You can always reaffirm and encourage them but stick to your guns and don't let them push you into giving in with their whining, crying, fits of rage or complaining.

My daughter loves this show on television called *The Dog Whisperer*, in which the host Cesar Milan goes into people's houses and helps them deal with noncompliant dogs. His solutions are always about the owner and rarely about the dog itself. Most of the time, it is the energy the owners are giving off that the dogs pick up on. Dogs and kids alike run in packs in that they follow the dominant person in the room, and there always has to be a pack leader for them to follow.

You have to be the pack leader to your kids. Once you have that calm assertive energy that you are in control, then they will feel it and eventually fall into line.

Do not get emotionally caught up in their behaviour. If you feel that anything they say or do is triggering you, then take a small timeout and confront them again once you have control. If you let your children know what your triggers are, then they will use them against you to control you. Use the self-control that God gave us to walk away but do not give in.

Remember, your children are not your enemies, so do your best not to treat them that way. If they don't want to give you the respect you deserve, then it's up to you to take these simple steps in a quietly confident way to show them that you are the one in charge.

NONCOMPLIANCE IN ADULTS

Sometimes when non-compliant children grow up, they become non-compliant adults. They might have jobs and friends like a normal adult, but when it comes to helping around the house or doing their fair share of duties for the family, they shut down.

Just like children, they will do the job so badly in hopes that they'll never be asked to do it again. Some of them just won't do it at all.

Many husbands are like this, coming home from work and just wanting to lie around on the couch instead of doing their part of the housework. As well, they want to avoid meaningful interaction with their kids or their community. They feel like it's enough for them just to work, and it's too much to ask for them to do anything else with their lives.

The partners of non-compliant adults have to be careful not to slip into the parent role with them. It becomes difficult to make them take on the adult role. If privileges are taken away by force, it may put the non-compliant adults into the role of disobedient children.

How do we draw them out of this state where they just want to earn money and not have any other responsibilities in the home?

Everyone does personal things for their partners. The partner of the noncompliant adult can just stop doing those things if they do not live up to their side of the bargain. What you withhold or do not do, however, should be in relation to what they refuse to take part in.

I disagree if you were to withhold intimacy from your partner if they didn't do the dishes. Instead, withhold your cooking. Only cook for yourself and then do your own dishes. Make your noncompliant partner cook and clean up for themselves. If they refuse to do their own dishes, then leave those dishes on their bed at night. These are called **natural consequences**.

These consequences will almost certainly trigger the noncompliant person into an angry response. Whatever you do, do not get on the escalator. You already know that the consequences will be bad no matter how much you argue. You can't run down the escalator of anger to get to a resolution. In that moment, you have to be assertive with your actions without getting drawn into a fight.

The partner of the noncompliant adult is not taking a role of power but is just removing themselves from the flow of activity so that the task that isn't done naturally affects the non-compliant adult.

Another example is when one of my clients had faulty brakes on her car. Her semi-mechanic husband told her that he would put the new brakes on himself. Weeks passed, and although she kept mentioning it, he would not act.

After going through the steps, she took the car to the mechanic herself and gave her husband the bill. When he got upset that another man had touched his car, she gently but firmly stated her case and walked away.

I am not saying that we should punish our partners, but we have to be assertive and firm in dealing with this type of adult. I do the following prayer when dealing with non-compliant people who have realized their pattern and want to be free from it.

PRAYER FOR NONCOMPLIANCE

LORD JESUS,
As a child, I often used the win-lose method to avoid any task that I didn't want to do. I would use aggressive anger, excuses, delays, arguing and withdrawing to get my way. I forced my parents to ask me so many times to do a task that finally they would just do it themselves. I knew that if I did a partial task or did it poorly, they would just take over.

My lack of compliance allowed me to control my interactions. I now realize that I have brought this pattern into my marriage. My spouse feels manipulated and abused by this passive-aggressive behaviour of non-compliance. My spouse is fed up with my patterns.

Because of these patterns, I have shallow relationships with my children. They fluctuate from seeing me as 'poor dad' to hating me for not being the adult father they need. I acknowledge that my hidden agenda of non-compliance has wounded many people.

I have hit a time of despair at the thought of losing my family. I ask you, Jesus, to touch me now with Your truth .I am ready to be the person that you created me to be – an adult who acts like an adult and not a child. I want to be free of the selfishness and laziness that my non-compliant behaviours dictate. Help me to put my spouse and my children before my own desires.

AMEN.

1 Corinthians 13:11 – "When I was a child, I talked like a child, I thought like a child, I reasoned like a child. When I became a man, I put childish ways behind me."

1 Peter 5:2-3 – "Be shepherds of God's flock that is under your care, serving as overseers – not because you must, but because you are willing, as God wants you to be; not greedy for money, but eager to serve, not lording it over those entrusted to you, but being examples to the flock."

10. LEVELS OF COMMUNICATION

Understanding the Patterns of Communication

There are different levels of communication between partners when each takes on or are given three basic kinds of roles:

- *In the adult role,* the individual takes responsibility for their actions in a mature way. This is the ideal role in healthy marriages.

- *In the parent role,* one partner assumes responsibility for both. There is a certain quality of dominance in the parent role.

- *In the child role,* the individual takes little or no responsibility for their part in the workings of the relationship in both practical and romantic senses. They want or are forced to take on a submissive role.

Example 1: The Princess Bride

Robert and Mary fell in love at a young age. Robert loved the way Mary looked at him, like he was her knight in shining armour. He had always dreamed of rescuing the princess, riding in on his white horse to save her from the dragon that threatened her.

Ten years later, Robert was no longer so impressed with his princess wife. She refused to learn how to drive, to use her education, to work in her profession or to take responsibility for anything beyond the mundane housework. Robert imagined that she would grow into the queen that he wanted alongside him, but instead, her desire was to keep the child role.

Eventually, he ended up becoming like her parent, ordering her around and snapping at her whenever he was displeased. His anger at the role he had been given was causing regular splashes, so he came to me for counselling. His other concern was that their children were disrespecting their mother and putting her in the child role as well, a consequence of seeing their father do the same.

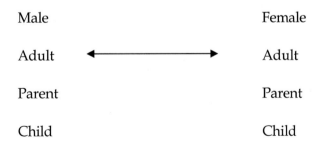

Good communication occurs when both partners assume equal adult roles and develop mutual respect for one another as an adult.

Mary does not want to claim equal responsibility as an adult and relinquishes responsibility of her life to Robert in the adult role, who really wants equal partnership. (Example: Robert is forced to drive his wife around.)

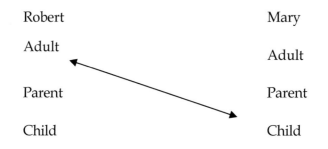

Robert	Mary
Adult	Adult
Parent	Parent
Child	Child

The resentment grows on both sides as Robert wants Mary to be his equal, but she wants to be taken care of. When Robert began to set boundaries and firmly insisted that she get her driver's licence, the relationship started to change. Mary felt more self-confidence, and Robert was relieved of the pressure of being the parent to his wife.

Example 2: The Momma's Boy

Another common role differential scenario occurs when one adult forces the other to assume the child role because they want to be the parent in the marriage.

Vic and Sonya were married at a young age after she got pregnant in high school. Vic went from being cared for by his mother to being cared for by his new wife, Sonya. He went from being spoiled by his parents to wanting to be spoiled by his new bride. In their first years of marriage, Vic compulsively bought big-ticket items, like cars, without discussing it with Sonya.

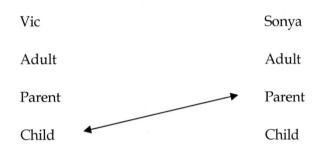

Vic	Sonya
Adult	Adult
Parent	Parent
Child	Child

These actions invalidated his responsibility, and Sonya took over as the parent. Sonya assumed that Vic (in the child role) needed to be cared for and supervised. This transfer led to the eventual invalidation of Vic's position of responsibility. Sonya would commonly remark, "I have three kids and my big kid — my husband."

Vic's resentment built up inside of him as stored anger. He self-medicated with liquor and food until he was very overweight. Sonya became angry at his passive-aggressive withdrawal and turned into a nag, expressing her anger through constant hounding.

In counselling, I instructed Vic to get his own bank account and to start making decisions for himself. Sonya had to learn to let go of Vic and concentrate more on her own happiness instead of taking care of him all the time.

Example 3: The War for Control

My wife and I fall into this pattern all too often, and if left unchecked, it can be very destructive. In my life, I grew up in extreme poverty and never knew where the next meal was coming from. By 17, I was on my own and had nothing. This insecurity developed a fear within me about falling back into poverty. I would take risks with money and did not trust anyone with my resources.

MaryBelle feels like I am trying to be the parent in our relationship with money. In her mind, she knows how to run our finances as good as or better than me and sees my fear as destructive towards our future wealth. She wants to take the parent role to loosen my tight grip on our funds.

Male	Female
Adult	Adult
Parent ←——————→	Parent
Child	Child

Both of us are trying to adopt the parent role as we do not trust each other's judgment with money. There are constant battles about spending, bank statement and future investments. We end up bickering about unimportant matters regarding specific purchases that are negligible considering the fact that, although we are not rich, we have been blessed.

In our lives, we still need to work on seeing each other as adults and giving each other the respect and space that is due. My wife needs to understand that I am still working through my fear issues with money, and I need to let her have more freedom and trust her decisions with our finances.

Taking the adult role is your responsibility, first and foremost. We cannot make people change or take roles that they refuse to take, but we can change ourselves. Setting boundaries, being firm and encouraging each other are the best ways to help them change their roles as well.

HEALING PRAYER FOR PATTERNS OF COMMUNICATION

LORD JESUS,

I have identified that, in my family, there is a problem with the way that we communicate. I, _____, have fallen into the pattern of being a _____ to my spouse, who falls into the pattern of _____, rather than being equals and both of us relating to one another as <u>adults</u>. Allow us, as marriage partners, to openly talk about this and come to an agreement that this is a faulty way of communicating and that it has caused great harm to our marriage and our family.

I pray that You, Lord, will give us wisdom and insight into what caused us to relate in this negative way and the strength to make positive changes so that our marriage can be a source of happiness and contentment. I ask forgiveness for any harm that I may have caused my spouse and children for placing myself and him/her in those roles. Help me to be an instrument of change for us all.

AMEN.

Intimacy

The subject of intimacy can be contentious and, in my experience as a counsellor, is often the elephant in the room when dealing with anger issues. As Christians, we feel ashamed to talk about intimacy and ignore the anger we feel until it splashes out in other areas.

I will only deal with a few of these issues in this book to give you an idea of some of the negative patterns that we might have concerning intimacy.

I have had several clients come to me whose relationships were breaking apart because of what was happening in the bedroom. One partner or both have been wounded in their past, and that can affect their intimacy with their partners.

Passive Aggressive Avoidance in Intimacy

This issue is commonly found in men, but women may have signs of it as well. Often men want women in a physical way, but because of their own emotional and spiritual insecurities, they cannot relate on an emotionally intimate level.

Craig never felt accepted by his mother. She divorced his dad and then treated Craig like he was an extension of his father, abusing him with insults and ignoring him. This deep emotional scar started to reflect itself in the way he acted around other women. He would want to be close to them but could not let himself open up and be vulnerable because he was afraid they would hurt him like his mother had.

When he married Katherine, things seemed alright at first, but she soon wanted more from him emotionally. He provoked her after sex through distant actions or by being critical. Katherine would lose her temper in response to his crass comments when she just wanted to be close to him, and that gave Craig even more reason to stay distant.

During intercourse, he perceived Katherine as an object in order to keep that "safe" distance. When she wanted him to be emotionally vulnerable, he provoked her until she became angry, at which point he could judge her as "crazy" and remain distant from her. This justified his own emotional emptiness. He could still be physically intimate without becoming emotionally or spiritually connected to his partner.

This pattern of mixed messages was repeated in many different forms, and in order to get past it, Craig had to deal with his mother issues and open up to Katherine. First, he had to admit that he had an issue and tell Katherine about it. Once she understood his problem, they were on the same page and could continue to work through that distance to become truly intimate.

Passive Aggressive Avoidance in Sexuality

Karen was sexually molested by her uncle when she was 10 years old. This deep wound in her spirit never healed, and although she managed to maintain an outward façade of health, inside the very idea of penetration disgusted and made her feel cold and separated from herself.

Karen wants her husband Rick spiritually and emotionally, but because of her sexual trauma, she cannot desire him in a physical way. After she is physically intimate with Rick, she hates herself and transfers that shame onto Rick.

To deal with her own guilt, she provokes him whenever he wants to be physical with her so that they have a big fight. At that point, Karen can justify to both of them why they can't be intimate. If he has hurt and wounded her, then she has a right to refuse his advances.

Karen can hold onto her lack of physical intimacy because she has created conflict. She remains distant and calm as her husband remains frustrated in his isolation and rejection.

Karen needs to heal those wounds before she can deal with her anger. After she has gone through the process with a professional, she needs to bring Rick into her circle of trust so that he can fully understand why all this is happening.

Many anger issues between partners are not because of deep-seated wounds from their past but because of laziness and ignorance. I call it "romantic ignorance."

Romantic Ignorance

We all need to sharpen up on our romance novel love skills. Too many husbands assume that once they are married, they don't have to pursue romance any longer. They feel like they have won the battle and assume that, for the next 40 years, they can sit back and enjoy the spoils of their victory. What they don't realize is that they are spoiling their own chances at happiness.

So if you haven't done anything romantic lately to win your wife over, guys, then this is the wake-up call to get out there and do something that makes her see how much you love her!

I think it goes for women too, though. So many wives give up on their love life after they have kids, not realizing that they are denying both partners an important part of their relationship. That being said, husbands need to open their eyes to see that their wives have taken on so much extra work caring for the home and their children. At the end of the day, they are completely exhausted and sex is the last thing on their minds.

All of us need to sharpen those skills, and the only way to do it is through practice. When couples continue dating after marriage, it builds shared romantic experiences and excitement.

One of the best ways to connect in an intimate way is to let yourself be vulnerable in front of your partner. Many men have a hard time letting themselves be open to their partners, but it builds an incredible amount of trust between the two of you. Trust is the wick for the flame of love; without it, there can be no fire.

Emotional awareness and openness increase intimacy. Looking at who you are as an emotional creature may be frightening. The reality is that both men and women are responsible for knowing their feelings and expressing them in a genuine way.

Active affirmations are more effective than passive connections. To be verbally encouraging is better than assuming that your partner knows of your love. "You look beautiful, honey" is an active affirmation, while a passive connection is to just assume that by not being critical you are stating that she is beautiful. You might think, "She's with me, so she already knows that I think she's beautiful or I wouldn't be with her." This kind of passive reliance on an unspoken connection always falls short. Be active in your love.

I find that few couples provide a safe place to be flawed. They never feel like they can "let their hair down." When you commit yourself to someone you love, then you are really telling them that sometimes it's okay to be yourself, warts and all. This goes back to the feeling of warmth we all get when giving and receiving unconditional love.

What I'm talking about is **Grace**. That's the action of giving your partner that extra leeway when they go off track and for loving them even despite their ugly parts. I know it isn't easy, but we all need that kind of acceptance, and there is no better place to start than right here, right now.

Ephesians 5:31-33 – "For this reason, a man will leave his father and mother and be united to his wife, and the two will become one in flesh. This is a profound mystery, but I am talking about Christ and the church. However, each one of you also must love his wife as he loves himself, and the wife must respect her husband."

Ephesians 5:28-30 – "In the same way husbands ought to love their wives as their own bodies. He who loves his wife loves himself. After all, no one ever hated his own body, but he feeds and cares for it, just as Christ does the church".

1 Corinthians 7:5-6 – "Do not deprive each other except by mutual consent and for a time so that you may devote yourselves to prayer. Then come together again so that Satan will not tempt you because of your lack of self-control. I say this as a concession, not as a command."

PRAYER FOR INTIMACY IN MARRIAGE

LORD JESUS,
I know that so often I let my anger and frustration at the world carry itself into the bedroom so that my spouse and I suffer from issues with intimacy.

It just seems easier to punish _____ than to be open and honest at my failings in the world. Help me to be a better person here at home, to put as much energy into my relationship with my spouse as I do with my co-workers and friends. I sincerely want to put _____ first, his/her feelings, wants and desires. Give me confidence to be vulnerable, to tell my spouse about my fears and failings. Protect me too, Lord, so that I feel safe in doing so. Help me to understand that we are not enemies but doing battle in this world on the same team.

I pray that I can truly live out Your commandment to love _____ as I love myself. Show me times when I need to affirm and bless my spouse and let me be confident that he/she will respond to my love. Make me be an encourager in my marriage, filling both of us with hope and joy for the future.

AMEN.

11. No Condemnation

The phone rings while I'm watching television with my son. Things are such a huge mess that I don't know how we are ever going to get out of this one as a family.

Three weeks ago, Hazel ran away. She went to school and, at the first break, walked away, meeting her Ecuadorian boyfriend at the bus station and then dropping off the face of the earth.

She had told her friends that she was sick of being judged by everybody. A girl had just told her in Bible class that she was going to Hell because she questioned whether everything in the Bible was true. The teacher had not only kept silent, but his stare was just as condemning.

Things were no better with us at home. A girl in her class had told on her for smoking cigarettes, and one of her friends had ratted her out for drinking. We had been having screaming matches every night for weeks over her behaviour.

One night, I finally lost it; my pail was overflowing and splashed when she threatened to run away. I fell into my old patterns of silence and moved a chair in front of her door, sitting there in my own negative stored emotions all night, waiting for her to make a move.

Then my baby was gone. Just like that. There was a rumour they had a gun. We feared the worst. She had been listening to Nirvana for months and idealized Kurt Cobain for taking his own life. Her boyfriend had been planning the escape for weeks. She had gone out of the school on a break and, within an hour, was on a bus into the unknown.

For the next few days, we exhausted ourselves and any resources we had to try to find her and bring her back home. My wife and I were at each other's throats, blaming each other. In desperation, we had called her older siblings for support. John, feeling helpless in Canada, left university to come back to Ecuador to look for her.

A Christian parent's greatest fear was realized in our home. Our 15-year-old youngest daughter had run away with a reckless boy and we could not find her.

Initially, in my panic and shame of her running away, I planned on finding her and taking her by force back to Canada. I had even considered putting her in one of those Christian boot camps where they break the spirits of rebellious teens.

My wife was threatening to leave me if I even tried something like that. Our son convinced us that if we wanted to have any sort of relationship with her in the future, then we had to let her go and come back on her own.

Through diligent work and I believe God's guidance, John sought out friends and enemies, and gathered clues to where she might be. He left by himself with a small backpack on a bus into the night, meandering down the coast of Ecuador until he found her trail.

Miraculously, he not only found her but managed to convince her to come back home if she wanted to. They spent a few days reconnecting, with John assuring her that the door home was always open. With a hug, he left them both behind and came back with the news.

At Christmas, the whole family planned on coming back. We were all hoping that Hazel and José would be joining us, but I still had my doubts.

MaryBelle picks up the phone before I get to it. She's been sleeping and thinks that it's our older daughter, Brandy, who is coming in by plane tomorrow.

"Brandy, is that you?" MaryBelle sleepily asks into the phone.

"No Mom, it's me, your other daughter. Hazel."

MaryBelle starts crying, so I pick up the other line.

"José and I are at the bus station. We're here in Quito. We are coming home. If we take a cab there, will you pay for it? We have no money, and we're so hungry."

The tears roll down my face freely. The prodigal daughter I had lost has been returned to me.

My daughter who I thought was dead is alive. Praise be to God.

Taking Care of Our Body

As Christians, we are all a part of the body of Christ. What is our "body of Christ" language telling the world? How are we communicating His love and forgiveness with all the broken people that need it the most?

More importantly, how are we communicating that love to ourselves?

There is another area that we seldom look at when talking about splashing, but I think we, as Christians, need to be specifically aware of it. We consider the spiritual realm to be a major part of our lives. There are spiritual splashes of anger. We need to discuss how to recognize them and realize the damage that they can do.

The children of ministers will find sermons directed at their "bad" behaviour. An authority in the church might mention sins that "certain" people should be ashamed of when everyone knows exactly who they are talking about. Other times, the religious authority will be pleading with God publically for the person to "see the light" of their ways. Have you ever found yourself in a fight or disagreement with someone and then had that person pray to God in a negative way about you?

All of these instances are spiritual manipulations used to attack others in anger. We have to start seeing these things for what they are if we are going to heal.

Using Prayer as a Tool of Anger

In the Book of Matthew, Jesus is asked how we should pray. He said that we should be praying in private with the door closed. I believe that this verse was given to us to prevent us, as sinners, from using the sacred communication with God to manipulate, shame or showboat.

> *Matthew 6:6* – "But when you pray, go into your room, close the door and pray to your Father who is unseen. Then your Father, who sees what is done in secret, will reward you."

Many of us are guilty of this in some way or another, and we have to give each other forgiveness in this area. Grace is needed when we use personal verbal communication with the Almighty for our own agenda. Only He can judge what a person's motives are.

When these prayers are born from negative emotional anger, it becomes abuse and must be recognized as such. Using "God" to condemn people that we are angry with for personal reasons is a blight on the church. We, as a community, must work together to set boundaries and stop this kind of thing from happening.

Pastors that Use Their Authority Blindly

The doctrine of some churches allows the authorities to go into people's lives and make decisions for them. These rules are arbitrary and, at times, can be manipulations of Scripture, used as tools of power held over the heads of believers.

It is disturbing when the pastor of a church has been given the authority to say who can and cannot get married. In other cases, how can a pastor determine what someone can do with their money or what business decisions they should be making?

Pastors are there to guide their flocks spiritually but not to make their decisions for them. This is just blatant use of their power to control others. This pattern is common in cults and should be treated with scrutiny. Jesus gave us the freedom to make our own choices and giving up that control is not in accordance with the way he wants us to live our lives.

A client of mine went to his pastor two years after his divorce to talk about moving on. He wanted to start dating again and was seeking advice about God's wisdom. The pastor, however, forbade him to date anyone else, quoting Scripture in the process. This moment added stored anger to my client's pail. He couldn't understand how he was supposed to live the rest of his life alone just because his wife had left him. He left the church and still has not gone back.

When spiritual outbursts take place, they can often cause the people who are suffering and looking for comfort to lose faith in the church and break away from the community. I can't tell you how many people I've counselled that have left the church for this very reason.

We are to love one another in the body of Christ, but using positions of power to control what others think and do will only add negative stored emotions to our collective pails.

Judgments Can Hurt Christian Parents

The devil can cleverly use Scripture to make parents feel guilty. A verse that is often quoted by writers and teachers is **Proverbs 22:6**: "Train up a child in the way he should go, even when he is old he will not depart from it." This line can be used to accuse and wound already hurting parents.

Satan's lie is that because you have not been good parents, your children didn't turn out "right." He tells parents that they have failed. There is enough logic in Satan's accusation to drive even fairly strong Christians to experience heavy guilt and shame.

The fundamental mistake so many parents make is to believe the enormous lie implicit in Satan's twisted logic. They believe that they have passed on a generational sin when, in fact, it was their child's choice to take the path they wanted.

What is the lie? That **children become godly when correctly raised by their parents** ... this is simply **NOT TRUE**. Everyone makes up their own minds, whether they choose to follow in their parent's footsteps or not.

Every person is free to choose their own path and only by choosing God's way do they become godly in their own lives. No parent can control their child's actions or their eventual godliness.

If we don't stop internalizing our children's actions, we will be filling our pail with anger.

Beware of Prophets that Want Your Money

It breaks my heart to see the wounded, the suffering and the lost—the people that Jesus lived with and was the most tender toward—leave the family of God because they are being spiritually abused.

Seven people from a single congregation came to me, all spiritually abused by a supposed "prophet." Three of them have since left the church for good. The other four are in long-term counselling. This prophet used his gift to extort money from them, seduce them sexually and cripple them emotionally with his words. Minimal charges were laid against this prophet, and he moved to another province in Canada and has reinstated himself as a prophet in a new church.

You can easily recognize false prophets because their egos take the place of their caring for the people in their flock. They want to control the hearts and minds of all the people that believe in them, taking away their free will in the name of prophecy. They use God's word to put fear into people to follow them or suffer the consequences. Their focus is not centred on compassion but on gaining more money, more power and more followers. Many times, they are sexually involved with several members of the congregation who fall under their spell of charisma and personal power.

When Jesus was tempted by Satan, it was to give up his free will so that he could have more power. Jesus refused Satan's temptations and we, as Christians, must also guard our choices from these wolves in sheep's clothing.

If not, our pails will be filled with false hope that will quickly curdle into shame and self-hatred for following a man instead of following God.

2 Corinthians 3:4-7 – "Such confidence as this is ours through Christ before God. Not that we are competent in ourselves to claim anything for ourselves but our competence comes from God. He has made us competent as minsters of the new covenant- not the letter but of the Spirit; for the letter kills but the Spirit gives life."

Do Not Follow Blindly

The false prophet's gifts may be powerful, but he uses them to manipulate others. He truly is the wolf in sheep's clothing. Our church body is not properly trained to identify these imposters. God wants us to be as gentle as doves but as shrewd as snakes. We are not to follow blindly no matter how powerful the gift of the preacher, teacher or prophet in front of us.

This kind of faith in other humans happens because we listen to other people's interpretations of the Bible and the teachings unquestionably. We are told that it is wrong to ask questions or doubt the teaching of our leaders.

It is never wrong to ask questions, and we must open our eyes to see the rationale behind the teaching. If love is not central in the teaching, then is it from Jesus? If we don't question, then we will find ourselves in the middle of spiritual abuse and that will lead to more anger.

The Fire of God is Love, Not the Burning Torch of Condemnation

The new life is found in breaking our chains to subjective regulation and finding freedom in the love of Jesus. The things that we need to find peace are choices and not mandates. This makes us empowered to take control of what we want in our lives without the fear of not doing exactly what other people want us to do.

> *John 1:8-10* – "If we claim to be without sin, we deceive ourselves and the truth is not in us. If we confess our sins, he is faithful and just and will forgive us our sins and purify us from all unrighteousness. If we claim we have not sinned, we make him out to be a liar and his word has no place in our lives."

Jesus set us free, and it is your choice whether or not you want to follow a set of rules or arbitrary regulations. Christ gives us confidence in ourselves and the path we choose. That confidence will help us relieve the fires of negative anger and be strong in our convictions.

We Are All Yucky! But He Still Wants Us

As full as your pail might be with all the sin and shame of past wounds, there is good news. Jesus' love is not determined by how messy your life is or how full your pail is. He sees through all that and, with his unconditional love, encourages us to keep moving towards healing.

THERE IS NO CONDEMNATION!

One of the repeated messages that Jesus brought to people was the insistence that we should not judge one another. For some reason, this message has been forgotten by His followers. Too often, we find ourselves condemning people, saying that they will go to Hell for are committing grievous sins.

Galatians 5:1 – "It is for freedom that Christ has set us free. Stand firm then, and do not let yourselves be burdened again by a yoke of slavery."

Romans 7:6 – "But now, by dying to what once bound us, we have been released from the law so that we serve in the new way of the Spirit, and not in the old way of the written code."

Yet we are supposed to take the plank out of our eyes before we look at the speck in our neighbours. We are only to look at our own pails and not continue to peer into the murky depths of our neighbour's pails.

This message is obvious, but we must also remember not to condemn ourselves either! Once we accept Jesus into our hearts, He is there to stay. He has paid for our sins with his life and set us free. We can see all the terrible things that we have done and the things that have been done to us, but that does not mean that we are doomed for it.

Be Free!

Our confidence comes from Christ instead of the law of the Old Testament.

> *Romans 8:1* – "Therefore there is now no condemnation for those who are in Christ Jesus, because through Christ Jesus the law of the Spirit of life set me free from the law of sin and death."

The Spirit of Life sets me free. The pressure is off! The law of the Old Testament tells me that I have to be perfect, but Jesus says that I am worthy of love just as I am. We are released from the old law to the new way of the Spirit.

What is the "Spirit of Life"?

The Spirit of Life is to be free to respond to life's challenges without fearing judgement because we have already surrendered our direction to Christ.

Romans 13:8 – "Let no debt remain outstanding, except the continuing debt to love one another, for he who loves his fellowman has fulfilled the law."

What Do We Have to Do? Love One Another

We are commanded to first and foremost **love one another**.

Open your hearts to people without desire to get anything from them; just love without reason or expectation of return. Unconditional love is like a beautiful plant that once rooted, spreads into all parts of our lives.

Don't Obsess, Just Do Your Best – Performance Orientation

As Christians, we are so often caught up in performing for other people's approval and love. That constant need to perform adds negative emotion to our pails and to the pails of those who love us because rarely do we measure up to the standards we set for ourselves and others.

This need to be in control of every aspect of our lives quickly fills our pails with anxiety as things seldom go as planned. We become fearful of doing anything at all and project our expectations onto others. This negative loop is so obviously destructive but is so easy to get caught up in it.

In Scripture, Jesus instructs us not to worry about what will happen tomorrow for it will take care of itself. God has a plan for us and trying to control each and every moment of our lives will start fires that were not there before.

This does not mean that we should not do our best in all things. Every action can be seen as a prayer in praise to

God, and when looked at from that perspective, it should make you want to excel in whatever you are doing.

On the flip side, when we screw up, God is not going to be there booing. He will pick us up gently in His arms of love and restore our spirits.

James 4:13-17 – "Now listen, you who say, 'today or tomorrow we will go to this city or that city, spend a year there, carry on business and make money.' Why? You do not even know what will happen tomorrow. You are mist that appears for a little while and then vanishes. Instead you ought to say, 'If it is the Lord's will, we will live and do this or that.' As it is, you boast and brag. All such boasting is evil. Anyone then, who knows the good he ought to do and doesn't do it, sins."

Matthew 6: 34 – "Therefore do not worry about tomorrow, for tomorrow will worry about itself. Each day has enough trouble of its own."

What is Your Life?

A favourite phrase of mine to use with those who have lost the joy of life and are driven by fear, doubt and worry is to "stop doing life and start living life."

To *live* life and not *do* life, we need to receive Christ's unconditional love. When we receive Christ's unconditional love, we can give unconditional love without condemnation.

The Good We Ought To Do Is LOVE!

PRAYER FOR HEALING FROM SPIRITUAL ABUSE

LORD JESUS,
When _____
(incident) happened, I felt that the rug had literally been pulled out from under my feet. I trusted _____, that God might be speaking to me through this person, so I became vulnerable and trusting. And then the betrayal was so deep and so personal that I felt I might never recover and trust You again. My spirit was crushed, and I wanted to run away from church, from other Christians and from You. I am so thankful, Lord, that You do not run away from us, but You continue to pursue us, even when we turn away.

Thank You for calling me back to a position of trust again. I pray that You will help me to see that what happened was man's sin and not Your abandonment of me. Help me to put this incident in perspective and to not let it shadow my life and my faith. Help me to truly forgive _____ and to let these painful memories go so I can move ahead in my faith and in my relationship to You and to the body of Christ.

Lord, if I have knowingly or unknowingly rained condemnation on one of my brothers or sisters in Christ, I ask that I be forgiven and perhaps given the opportunity to make amends. I pray for a loving and humble heart that does not judge and condemn but sees people through Your eyes, with love and compassion.

AMEN.

12. Emptying Our Pails

The counselling session just ended and I need a break. My client had broken down when we were talking about forgiving her father for past abuses. The session had hit too close to home, and I can feel the painful memories flooding back in.

I slip into the chapel, the pew is hard against my back which feels riddled with knots of stress. The solace of the empty chapel brings peace into my turbulent mind. So much has happened in the past few years that it's hard to keep track of it all.

We moved as a family back to Edmonton, and I had to start over from scratch. Our mission experience had drained us physically, emotionally, spiritually and financially. I had been forced to go back to teaching but, with the encouragement of my family, had started my own counselling practice.

Within a year, I gave the first anger management course right here where I'm sitting. Since then, God has used me to help so many people and I sometimes forget that it was me who needed the same healing many years earlier.

Back then, I didn't even know I had a pail, let alone that it was full to the brim. It had been several years since being born again, and my marriage, which I thought had been saved with me, was falling apart. I was angry at God for not giving me the strength to erase all my bad patterns and stored anger from the past.

In that low point, I was searching for some way of releasing the pressure of my full pail. There was a healing conference in this church, and instead of doing the usual yard work, I decided to attend. Really, in my mind, I was doubting if anything could save me or my family from the constant fighting.

The first day of the conference ended badly for me. I walked out of the healing process, right in the middle of the session. The speaker had been doing a visualization exercise where he asked us to walk through a garden, imagining it to be Heaven. We were to see Jesus, standing on a bridge over a gentle stream.

"There is someone on that bridge beside Jesus," the speaker continued. "That is the person you have to forgive."

Standing there beside Jesus was my father. My eyes had flown open, and I walked out of the church. I was not prepared to even think about him.

The last thing I wanted to think about was my dad, but there I was, drawn back that same evening to the healing conference. Something had to change; I felt ready to spill over the sides and burn up the world with my relentless anger.

The speaker spotted me and walked up with a smile. "Aren't you the one that walked out of the forgiveness session yesterday? I'd like you to sit with me and finish the exercise."

I was shocked that he remembered me, and the power of the Holy Spirit, I know now, brought me back to that moment. He started the visualization exercise again, walking me into the garden of paradise. Standing there is Jesus and beside him is my dad, the most loathed figure in my mind.

The vision seemed so real. My voice wavered as I started to talk to this man who I was sure I'd never see again, "Where are you, Dad?"

"I'm in Heaven, son. Jesus has made me whole." His smile was warm and welcoming.

A tidal wave of anger crashed through me in that moment. There was no way that this man who tortured me belonged in Heaven. It's just not fair that he gets eternal life after what he did to me. He needs to suffer like I've suffered. Why did he deserve to be in the arms of Jesus after all he had done?

Then, just as suddenly as it had come, the anger left and I felt completely empty. The realization that my dad was whole, complete and perfect in Heaven took hold and a new emotion filled the place of anger. Tears streamed down my face as I reached out to hug him. I knew that I would see him again when I went to heaven, and on that day, we would finally be together in peace.

The Holy Spirit was filling me, moving through me and, without words, asking me where I want to be healed. Some of the pain was too hard to let go, but little by little, I could feel the rage, hurt and shame drain away.

Empty of the fire and full of a peace that passes understanding, I fell back and floated down that stream. I was finally free of my hatred and anger towards Jack Thompson, my father. I was finally free to love without fear, to stand without shame and to walk forward into a new future.

But here I sit now, in the same spot, and feel a mix of relief and confusion. There are still stored emotions in my pail, but I have seen the way out.

Kneeling on the altar, I close my eyes and take myself back to the garden. It is time to forgive my dad again and be free.

HOW DO WE EMPTY OUR PAILS?

Even when you feel like you are at the bottom of a giant pail of pain, hurt and anger and that there is no way out, don't lose hope: forgiveness is the way. The filthy fluid that fills your pail may seem like it is impossible to scoop out, but forgiveness is the drain at the bottom of the pail.

All of the conflict resolution we have just learned is useless unless we start to really look at emptying our pails. That stored anger will continue to build up into internal pressure and the need to release it, most often through conflict, will continue. If we can't empty those pails, then we will continue to dance around with our negative expressions of anger and nothing will get better.

Embrace Change and Embrace Yourself

The first step is always to embrace change through the power of Jesus Christ. He gives us the freedom to wash our sins away and start a new life. We can drain our pails, we can change our patterns, and we can live without anger!

Once we see this, we have to keep on in the footsteps of Jesus and refuse to give up on ourselves just as He refuses to give up on us. There have been times in my life where I wanted to give up, when the pail was so full of disgusting filth that I thought it would be easier to walk away from everyone I love rather than deal with the mess that is me.

The truth is that we can't walk away from ourselves. The only real solution is to face our problem and walk towards the change. Our fire might be out of control now, but with time, patience and the grace of God, you will be a light unto the world so keep hope.

Admit That You Are Angry

Like most healing problems, we have to see the wound to bandage it up. Our natural inclination is not to look at the "blood" but to slap a bandage on it. The analogy continues: if we don't clean and purge the wound, then infection sets in. When you admit to yourself and your loved ones that you have an anger problem, you can start to change as a person.

Owning your anger issues and taking responsibility for your actions is a way to be free of it. You can only let go of something you own, and if you own your anger, then you can let go of it.

Can you do it? Can you really look at yourself in the mirror of truth and say, "I am an angry person? I am consumed with anger"?

It's painful, I know. For me, at first there were constant splashes and a fire burning out of control. It felt as if my whole world was going to collapse, and I just wanted to run away. I feared rejection and isolation once the anger stored in my pail was brought into the light.

Walk Toward the Pain

You can't run away from the pail; it's chained to you. The only escape is to walk towards the pain. The roots of anger sometimes run so deep and we have to be willing to dig them up. Often we cannot totally get rid of the past events that haunt us.

Have you ever had dandelions in your lawn? You might cut off the top, but they always came back. You need to dig them out by the roots to get rid of them. That takes time and patience. It is exactly the same way with the stored anger in our pail. If we scoop from the surface, we might drain it a bit, but until we look at the root of the issue, our pail will keep refilling.

If your mother abandoned you as a child, you may get down on your knees one night and forgive her. But that is only the first step, and unfortunately, life isn't that simple. The stored anger of that abandonment will keep resurfacing in other areas of your life.

Don't give up. Keep walking towards the pain as that is where the healing lies. There is always hope.

Expose the Roots to Yourself

Can you do it? Can you dig deep into your past to find the roots of your anger? Like uncovering a festering wound and exposing it to the air so that it can heal, it is better to do it now than postpone it any longer. The problem may be that you don't want to expose ugly truth that you think is better left hidden.

Every time I get up in front of an audience to share my story of abuse, I get so anxious at unveiling my ugly past that I want to run. I don't want these strangers to know how awful it was for me to grow up in a home full of anger and sin. What if people think less of me?

Well, *you* don't have to get up in front of people and empty your dirty pail, so you can relax. Your parent's right to privacy is just another tool to keep the shameful past bottled up. You only have to expose the roots to yourself and the closest people to you that it affects.

Like any filthy pail of flammable material, the longer it stays bottled up, the more toxic it becomes. When we finally splash with that anger, it can be explosive.

There is no reason to protect the people from your past that have hurt you. Your own admission and acceptance is the key to digging up those roots and draining your pail.

History Repeats Itself

Scripture talks about generational sin as we repeat the sins of our parents. This cycle must be examined and set free on both dramatic and subtle levels.

How many of us have suffered the abuse of angry parents and then married an angry spouse?

My findings over the last 20 years of counselling have indicated that about a quarter of the kids from angry homes become at least as angry as the parent with the worst issue. About half of the children marry into homes where anger becomes a major issue. A quarter of them learn to deal with the roots of anger and have normal marriages.

These numbers are not scientific, but it has been clear to me that we are leaving a legacy of anger and hate with our children.

Becoming the One You Hate

Too many victims of an angry parent become the very person they hated. We would like to hope that the boy that watches his mother get slapped around would hate any thought of violence. In my experience working with violent men, almost all of them watched their mothers get beaten at some point or another.

On a number of occasions, I have witnessed male or female children become just as abusive, if not more abusive, to their parents. In one family, all three daughters that were abused became abusive to their mom. It is sad to see the physical violence some of these children inflict on their parents.

Hope Drains the Pail

There is hope. We can open our eyes to the sickness and escape the cycle of anger. It only takes one person to wake up and realize that their education in relationships was not healthy. Once they realize that the way they treat their own relationships is not healthy, there is hope that change will take place.

My relationship with my father was beyond distant; it was hateful. The way he made me feel when he beat me was that I was never good enough to be his son. With my own son, I had incredibly high expectations of what he should be and was hard on him in everything he did.

One day, I woke up and realized how amazing my son is. It was at that moment that a new friendship started between us, as equals with mutual respect. We broke the cycle of hate and expectation, and if I can do it, then so can you. Our relationship is a work in progress, with both of us growing and changing through the years.

It is good to realize we have problems, but we need to let them go as soon as we can and move on. To be free is to realize that we don't have to conform to any pattern and that every day we can be a new person.

The process of change means letting go of the past and embracing the new transformation that can be found in Christ.

Where do we start? Where can I find the path to change my life?

Forgiveness is the first step on this new path to freedom.

FORGIVENESS IS THE WAY

Why forgive?

Jesus died on the cross so that all people can be forgiven from our sins. That includes me, my parents, you and the ones that have sinned against you. We all fall short, but the love of Jesus lifts us up to reach a new level here on Earth so that you don't have to wait for Heaven to be free from the nightmares of your past.

Being forgiven allows us to forgive others. It also helps us to forgive ourselves for all the hateful things that we have done and that have been done to us. If we don't forgive, there are too many negative consequences to face. We will continue to express anger, pain and hatred toward innocent people in our lives.

Without forgiveness, we try to control other people. We will be pressed down by stress and tremendous tension and will be resentful towards God for giving us this burden to bear. We will be ashamed. We will seek revenge.

No. There has to be a way to change. There must be a way to forgive.

If we analyze the things inside the pail, separate them and filter them out, and then forgive each and every offender one by one, the pail will gradually drain.

This is not an easy process. Maybe you've been called to the altar to forgive those who have hurt you. On your knees, you cried out in someone's arms when you forgave the people that had wounded you.

I hate to tell you this, but the hard truth is that *every day God is asking you up to the altar to forgive the ones that have hurt you.* Every day is a new day to confess and to be forgiven, to express and to give grace.

Some of these people have committed sins against you literally thousands of times. I don't think that trying to remember each and every one of them is productive or necessary. On the other hand, there are significant markers, moments and wounds that have to be dealt with one at a time to empty them from your pail. As they surface in your mind, you must give them up to God so that you can be free.

The bad thing about these intense psychological issues is that sometimes forgiving the wrongs that caused them once is not enough. Each time you feel anger, pain, regret, shame and sorrow about some instance of hurt, it must be forgiven again and again until it doesn't resurface. **The process of forgiveness is ongoing as long as the seed of anger remains.**

The most important thing to remember is that unresolved anger is literally buried alive in our pails. Anything that lives will grow and multiply. The anger needs to die, and just like Jesus died on the cross, you must die to roots of anger.

If you need guidance in forgiveness, make the prayers personal by rewriting them and making them your own. Find someone you trust to pray with, then sincerely say your prayer to the One that forgives. You may have to do it more than once. The harder that our hearts have become, the more we will resist the softening that is necessary.

> *Matthew 6:15-16* – "For if you forgive men when they sin against you, your heavenly Father will also forgive you. But if you do not forgive men their sins, your Father will not forgive your sins."

Prayers of Forgiveness

LORD JESUS,
I now know how important forgiveness is. It is the reason that You had to die on the cross. I need Your heart, first of all, so that I have the desire to forgive those who have hurt me. I pray for that desire. Soften my heart of stone. Today, I forgive _____ for the pain and suffering he/she has cost me in my life. I forgive this person for _____.
AMEN.

(Repeat for as many people/sins as you feel the need.)

LORD JESUS,
Having forgiven the people in my life for their sins against me, I am now ready to ask Your forgiveness for the sins I have committed against others. I know there are many. I ask You to bring them to my mind

now, so that I can be forgiven. Please forgive me, Lord, for the pain and hurt I have caused _____, for the sin of _____ in his/her life.

AMEN.

(Repeat for as many times as you need. This may take several sessions, as your heart softens and remembers.)

LORD JESUS,
I know that the pain I still feel does not mean that I have failed to forgive. I release Jesus to break the power of pain in my memories. I release _____ to be responsible to You, God. Thank You, Lord, for the fact that my forgiveness releases me from all the power of the evil one that came into my life with this sin. I thank You, God, that I no longer have to focus on past offenses. I thank You for the permission to live for today. I thank You for releasing thankfulness into my heart and that I can have a new freedom in my life.

AMEN.

LORD JESUS,
I receive Your forgiveness. I give up my desire to justify myself or prove I am right with _____. In Your name, I break all of the curses of sowing and reaping that could have come down into the next generation with this un-forgiveness. I ask that I be restored to a new relationship if it is safe to do so, and that I have a clean heart.

AMEN.

13. THE GOOD WE OUGHT TO DO . . .
(BUT USUALLY DON'T)

The cars keep coming into the church parking lot until it is fuller than I've ever seen it. I can't believe so many people are coming to support me through this nightmare.

One night, I woke up with a pain in my stomach. We went into the hospital and the x-ray showed a blockage. When they opened me up, they found my digestive system riddled with tumours. The cancer had been growing for years and was almost at the stage where, if we didn't cut it out, then it would be inoperable.

Three feet of my small intestines and 19 or more tumours later, I was still alive. John came home from China and Brandy from Indiana. The family gathered around, tight again in support. I was sure I was going to die.

For the first few weeks, it was touch-and-go as to how I was going to recover. The strength to go on had drained out of my spirit. As a family, we had somewhat bounced back financially, but now that I could no longer work, I was so anxious about money. *The old insecurities and fears about providing for my family came back into my pail.*

Then I found out that a night in the church had been planned for me. All the people I had counselled and helped with the anger management course, as well as my church family, were gathering around to support me.

Looking around the room, I can't believe how full it is of people that love me. A donation is taken up, and in just a few hours, we had enough money to make it through my recovery.

God is not done with me yet. I know that now as I stand here before the crowds of fellow Christians that are pouring their love and support down onto me.

Just when I needed them the most, they stepped up and did the good that they felt they ought to do. More than that, though, their love and encouragement filled my pail with a new hope and energy. I know that I'm going to beat this thing. The power of God is so much stronger than the power of death.

The message is clear and written on the smiling faces of my family, friends and those I have helped drain their own pails: the good we ought to do is love.

14. THE HOLY SPIRIT WHISPERS

So far we've learned to identify the anger stored in our pails, the negative patterns that destroy our peace, how to get off the escalator of anger by recognizing triggers, how to break abuse and, finally, how to resolve conflict.

What if I told you that most of these lessons are unnecessary if we just listen to the little voice in our heads?

You might scoff and not believe me, but I would bet you already know the answer to it in your heart and, more importantly, in your brain.

The surprising thing about the majority of people that I have counselled is that they already know what they need to do but go around waiting to be told anyways.

As Christians, we are in a unique place in which we are told about this whisper of inner knowledge and told to listen to it. We are given great wisdom without having to ask for it and that great wisdom is called the Holy Spirit.

When we ask Christ into our lives, He comes with his Spirit. What a gift!

God created the world then sent Jesus to save it. Everything Jesus did in the gospels demonstrated God's love for us. We are all chosen to be loving men and women of God. Love is an act of our will, not a feeling.

So what about the Holy Spirit? I've been to many churches that believe the Holy Spirit speaks through them in tongues and visions. That may well be true, but aren't we forgetting that the Spirit is with us every moment of every day, **quietly whispering to us about the good we ought to do?**

Please don't get this message mixed up with all the psychotic extremists that say there is a voice telling them to blow things up. No, the whisper that I'm talking about tells us one specific thing: **THE RIGHT THING DO TO.**

If that whisper talks about doing some external action like hurting, judging or convincing, then it probably isn't the Holy Spirit. The voice inside is only concerned with our own right actions.

Secularists call this inner voice our "conscience" and that is a fine word as well. I'm not here to argue semantics of the inner workings of our brains. Personally, I believe it is the Holy Spirit speaking to me about what I should be doing. Knowing that it is God speaking to me in a quiet voice gives it strength and purpose.

If you remember, in the first chapter we talked about **anger as a sign that change needs to happen.** True change can only take place from the inside out. Look around you and see all the people that want to change their partners, their families, their children, their churches, their communities and their world. They rarely see that true change only happens from the inside out.

The Holy Spirit that speaks through conscience is our gift from God. It leads us to do the good we ought to do. The Holy Spirit is there to help change one person only: the person that hears it.

What happens when we don't listen to the Holy Spirit speaking about right action?

We justify. It's that simple. As soon as we refuse to do the good we ought to do, we feel guilty, so then we must justify that guilt in order to live with ourselves.

How do we justify? By externalizing the guilt. We can't admit that we feel bad because we didn't do something we should have. Instead, we point the negative feeling outward at someone else. We inflate the faults of the other to make it easier on ourselves to feel this way.

We have just started a fire of conflict.

Let me give you an example:

Ben comes home from work and sees his wife, Alison, sitting on the chair with her head in her hands, looking dishevelled. He can immediately tell that she's had a bad day. He looks around and sees that the dishes haven't been done and supper is not started even though it is her turn.

A quiet but firm voice blows through his thoughts and says, "You should go to her and give her a hug and suggest that we order in. Then you should do the dishes and offer for her to lie down."

Ben knows that good he ought to do is ignore his own agenda and weariness because Alison needs his understanding and support. He has a choice:

a.   Do the good I ought to do and love my wife in an act of my will (doing the dishes).

b.   Ignore the call to do the right thing and justify my actions, externalizing the guilt.

Ben has had a rough day, too, and is tired. He had expected to have a small nap before enjoying dinner and then watching the football game. He ignores the nudge of the Holy Spirit.

The results:

• Ben begins to **justify his actions**: "I worked hard all day providing for this family and this was her night to make dinner. If I let her get away with it tonight, then she'll start expecting this every night. Next thing I know, she'll have control of me and I'll be her slave."

• Ben knows this isn't true, but he has already made a choice not to do the good he ought to do. Now he has to **inflate her faults** to justify the way he is thinking.

"She should be able to look after the house after her part-time job. That's nothing compared to what I do all day. She's making me feel guilty because she can't use her time properly. She's always so selfish when it comes to her work. I can't believe that she's trying to pull this off."

By ignoring the call of the Holy Spirit, Ben is preparing to do battle with his wife because of his externalized guilt. He makes some snide comment about how dirty the house is and starts angrily slamming around the dishes, trying to trigger her anger so he can feel that he is right in his choices.

Alison had a brutal day at work, getting in a big fight with her boss about something that wasn't her fault. She had a feeling that Ben might be angry with her if he came home to a dirty house, but after trying for an hour to clean, she just sat down to think about the day.

She feels her own anger bubble up as he starts to pull triggers. There is a quiet voice inside, though, also telling her the good she ought to do: "Ben probably had a hard day, too, and I know he was looking forward to the game tonight. I should just go and give him a hug, tell him about my day and suggest that we order in and watch the game together."

Alison chooses not to listen to the Holy Spirit telling her the good she ought to do. **She justifies her actions**: "He's lucky to have me. He thinks he works so hard, but my job is 10 times more demanding than his. The last thing I feel right now is respect for him. He deserves to miss his stupid football game. If he expects me to be some goodie goodie housewife, then he's got another thing coming."

Alison needs to **inflate his faults** and make him into a bad guy so that she can justify not listening to the Holy Spirit: "I can't believe I married such a jerk! He's just like my dad, totally blind to how much work I do. He thinks his life is so tough and complains all the time when really I do all the work around here. I wish people knew how inconsiderate he really is. What a lazy hypocrite."

Locked in the cycle of minimizing the other to justify their own failings, they both pull the trigger and jump on the escalator of anger. A fight and splash is inevitable.

They don't realize that love isn't just a feeling but truly an act of our will. Love isn't directed by the fancy of our feelings. The love God calls us to give is the love that is directed by the act of our will. In order to do this self-controlled love, we need to be obedient to the directions of the Holy Spirit.

Is the answer ever to accuse the other person about not doing the good they ought to do? We can recognize when someone is not doing the right thing, and it is so easy to start throwing stones. What did Jesus say about throwing stones?

John 8:7 – "If anyone of you is without sin, let him be the first to throw a stone at her."

What Jesus was talking about was that we need to concentrate on our own sins instead of throwing stones at other people. The truth of change is always to look inward at the love we ought to be doing instead of at how wrong everyone else is.

In every conflict, there are two parties involved. Society teaches us that the best way to resolve a conflict is to convince the other person that they are wrong and have them concede defeat. This system has led to divorce, violence and war between nations.

The only person we can change is ourselves!

If there is a conflict, then the first thing we need to do is stop transferring the guilt of our own failed actions (of NOT following the Holy Spirit) onto other people. The way forward is to admit to ourselves the place where we have failed.

What stops us from doing this? It sounds easy to say, "If I have a problem with someone, then I need to look at how I have failed first."

So why is it so hard? One word: **Pride**. We are all so proud that we can't even admit to ourselves that we have failed. To protect our fragile egos, we need to point the finger at someone else in order to alleviate that guilt.

When you finish reading this chapter, do not go back into your relationships and start pointing out how much other people don't do the good they ought to do. Don't tell your husband or wife how much they need to read this book because it is really *them* that needs to change. Open your eyes and see that true change only comes from the inside.

A well-known quote from Ghandi iterates the point: "You have to be the change you want to see in the world."

To me, as a Christian, that means that, in every situation, you should look in the mirror and ask yourself if you have listened to the whisper of the Holy Spirit.

Don't deny when you've been ignoring the promptings of the Holy Spirit. Simply say you are sorry and do not justify or explain why you did it. Be the change that you want to see. Let the Holy Spirit fill you with the LOVE that shows itself in actions.

If you do this, you can be free from the trapping of conflict that burn and scar the ones you love.

15. FREE AT LAST

The waves crash over the front of the boat soaking us both. I scream like a little girl with fear and excitement.

John grins beside me like a maniac. We are on a boat off the shore of Turkey, heading straight into a 10-foot swell and rocking around like we are on a roller coaster.

I don't know if I'm going to die or if I've ever felt more alive.

Looking down at my bare stomach, I see the long scar there and remember just how close I've been to the other side.

Four years after my cancer, my son convinced me that I should take a trip with him backpacking around Turkey and Greece to see the places I had always dreamed about going. He had been travelling the world for years and wanted to show me what it was like to have adventures on the road.

Here we were, laughing and yelling together, having the trip of a lifetime. Every day, something magical would happen that would leave us both in awe. We had become so much more than father and son; we were friends.

We had done it! I had broken the generational cycle of anger between father and son. We were finally free of those patterns of guilt, shame and stored anger.

The captain turned back for a cove to escape the big waves. As the sun set, John suggested that I should take the anger management course I had been teaching and make it into a book. He said that he'd even help me write it.

My life has not been easy. I have suffered through many things, and because of that, my pail was full of stored anger. With the grace of God and the wisdom given to me, I was able to release that anger and go back into the equilibrium with the fire that keeps me warm, lights my way and warns me of when things need to change.

If I can change, then so can you. Now go and be free of your anger. Go with all my blessings and all the blessings of those who love you.

There is freedom from the pain of the past, there is balance for your emotions, but most of all, there is grace to help us lift ourselves when we no longer feel the strength to go on.

May the Lord bless you and keep you, may His face shine upon you and give you strength. Go in peace and serve the Lord.

Amen.